Don't Call Me Old—
I'm Just Awakening!

Spiritual Encouragement for Later Life

Don't
Call Me
Old—

I'm Just

Awakening!

Marsha Sinetar

Paulist Press

New York/Mahwah, N.J.

Cover design by Cynthia Dunne
Book design by Saija Autrand, Faces Type & Design

Library of Congress Cataloging-in-Publication Data

Sinetar, Marsha.
    Don't call me old—I'm just awakening! : spiritual encouragement for later life / Marsha Sinetar.
        p.   cm.
    Includes bibliographical references and index.
    ISBN 0-8091-4097-7
    1. Christian aged—Religious life.   2. Christian aged—Conduct of life.   I. Title: Do not call me old, I am just awakening!   II. Title.

BV4580 .S55 2002
248.8′5—dc21

                                                    2002003848

Published by Paulist Press
997 Macarthur Boulevard
Mahwah, New Jersey 07430

www.paulistpress.com

Printed and bound in the United States of America

My beloved speaks and says to me:
"Arise, my love, my fair one,
and come away;
for, now the winter is past,
the rain is over and gone."

Song of Solomon 2:10–11

For friends,

Saundra T. Brewer

Betty Gaiss

Patty Murphy

Dee Roshong

Sister Florence Vales
Monastery of Saint Clare

Acknowledgments

Special thanks to three editors, Maria Maggi, Don Brophy, and Paul McMahon at Paulist Press, for faithful attention to the nuances and the "voices" in this project; to Della Dressler for expert, steadfast word processing; to Raymond J. Sinetar and Dan Raas, respectively, for sterling advice and counsel.

Such friendship. Such support. I am grateful. My heart is full.

Table of Contents

Introduction

~ Concerning the Yin and Yang
of "successful aging" ~

*. . . If one's old age is to be happy,
there must be a change of attitude.
And it is important that
this inner reformation should
take place early.*

Paul Tournier*

---

*Paul Tournier, *Learn to Grow Old* (New York: Harper and Row; London: SCM Press, 1972).

Introduction

Picture two friends who live far apart. They are old-fashioned letter writers and talk over their stuff of life by mail: Freely they discuss their creative struggles, career ups and downs, family matters—illness, healing, the birth of grandchildren—and their respective growth as individuals, especially along spiritual lines. And aging.

The following exchange of letters mirrors the uplift that I and my closest friends receive from one another. Over many years, mutual encouragement sustains the joys of our companionship. No matter where in the world we happen to be, we stay connected. Although I've fictionalized these long-distance friends, the content of their discussions is rooted in fact.

The material presented in this book initially came from research I conducted for a speech on aging for a "Who's Who"–caliber audience of gerontologists, health-

care professionals and life-care executives. While preparing, I worried about what I could say about aging that
they didn't already know. The upbeat nature of my talk
also concerned me. How can anyone be blithe about "old
age" given its apparent down side? Finally the truths of
my own spiritual experience kicked in. I recognized
another reality: ultimate Reality. I realized that whenever
we're inordinately dismal or fearful about aging, it means
we've neglected life's spiritual dimension—haven't rested
deeply enough in the peace that passes understanding[1]
to disengage from the gross materiality of existence.

Now I had my message. To the degree that we commune intimately with God, understand our oneness
with Absolute Reality, to that degree we enter into the
power and tender consolations of living Love. Later life
is wholly transformed by that spiritual hardiness, a
phrase I define as strength born of union with the divine
Love, or God of our understanding.

An "Opportunity Season"

Spiritual awakening, we are told by mystic author
Evelyn Underhill, is an elevation of consciousness
sparked by our conviction that we are more than "the
flesh," that God—or the highest life, power and intelligence—is at hand, and that we are somehow at one with

that life, that divine love. Spiritual awakening lifts so many sad moods linked to aging: melancholy; the anxiety born of our sense of mortality; our feelings of isolation. Awakening brings with it the certainty that "The Lord is our shepherd";[2] that we shall never want. Thus do we savor some bit of sublime imperishability while yet here, on earth.

Only this taste of the divine love restores us. It blesses "old age" with a lavish feel. The advanced years that once seemed so chilly now warm us—seem a "winter long past."[3] At our ground of being, we meet each day as an opportunity to align ourselves with the everlasting Reality that heals.

Thus my title: While to others, we may appear old—graying, dated, antique—in our heart of hearts, we're just realizing the joy, the beauty, the sacred depths of life. How ironic that what looks to the senses as "the end" of life is truly the beginning.

Aside from all the weightier theological benefits of, say, eternal salvation, if a more abundant existence isn't one of the best, most immediate rewards of a sincere spiritual life, I don't know what is. Spiritual awakening stirs our longing for the new—or the familiar—the untried, the "impossible dream." It heightens purpose. It motivates. It strengthens.

I shared all of that in my speech on aging. The audience's ebullient response to my theme of spiritual awakening encouraged each point. Their feedback was overwhelmingly positive. People flocked to the stage, telling me I'd been describing their ninety-year-old mother, father, or great-aunt. They voiced a palpable hunger for their own attributes of spiritual hardiness— courage, endurance, nobility of character, optimism in the face of challenge, and the like. They wanted to respond to events with the transformational mind they'd just heard about. They understood I was not talking about steps or formulas or some new doctrine, but a tried and true wholeness of thought that transforms all for the good.

Traveling back home after the talk, I realized my ideas about aging have been drastically transformed. Perhaps this is true for you, too. A quick review of recent TV programs or news reports will reveal that this shift has occurred in the collective mind: What most of us once considered "over the hill" has changed. For example, today my dearest friends and I discuss our lives in spiritual, not ageist, terms. We wonder aloud how to practice our virtues; how to walk—not just talk—our high standards. In this practice, everyone's path is unique, if also guided by overarching principles: genuine intent, loyalty to an elevated vision of possibility, the Golden Rule, the love of God. I've seen one friend make peace with a long-alienated family member. Another has cut her toxic familial cords. A third practiced "love of neighbor as self" by joining the Peace Corps when in her late sixties. A fourth friend nearing seventy started a new business after "retiring." We support each other's ambitions; our talks run along invigorating lines. Spiritual lines. We share verses of scripture. Exchange inspiring news stories. Send one another bits of poetry and even cartoons. Even when we're troubled about something at the *start* of a conversation, we end up cheerier because our understanding has evolved. In part, that's spiritual awakening: We're rethinking old, false assumptions. We're learning that when it comes to aging and ageist assumptions, *thoughts* are powerful influences. Thought, at its finest, is prayer. We're thinking more soundly, as Emerson once recommended, in order to yield ourselves to one sublime, perfect Whole.

By echoing that trusted dialogue, I aim to further both that yielding and that mutual support. The upcoming conversation, if fanciful, acknowledges feelings, and not simply theory. My fictionalized friends share metaphysical and prayerful techniques. Properly understood, these may enhance our later life's experience. "Awakening" is not just a solution to the problems of old age. It is *the* solution.

Dialogue As an Exchange of Selves

I ask you to envision the following imaginary composite: Two confidants, both bright, curious, and well-read. Theirs is an educative, mutually supportive correspondence—the sort of open dialogue that I've heard called an "exchange of selves." These two reveal their hopes and fears to each other. They diligently study whatever interests them. Each has at hand a library of books, selected periodicals and, of course, on-line resources. Each quotes directly from this data bank when exactness is desired. (Be assured that, in letters and e-mails, I and certain pals do quote, verbatim from books and news clips. The would-be scholars in our crowd do cite references, although I'm told this isn't the norm.) The coming dialogue is essentially a parable—a tale about everyday life from which deeper truths may be drawn. In this parable the moral is clear: Earthly life is our season of opportunity to know God—self-existent Life—and to accept the immutable Love so that we may live on, as promised in John 3:15, that they who receive the living Christ within shall never perish.

Just so you know, I kept in mind a loose psychological profile for these spiritual companions. First, please meet Bo—a.k.a. "B"—the practical executive and "applications" character. Bo hears an idea and rushes to use it concretely. "B's" solutions reflect a hearty appetite for popular notions about spirituality, the ones swirling around us in the news, in business and society. "B" is action oriented, so stays busy by *doing*. El, an eclectic writer-artist, is the more offbeat of the two. A lover of film, food, and metaphysics, El's joys flow from "being," and that mystical view sets up the trajectory for the friends' spiritual dialogue. El is firmly rooted in a transcendent reality, as anyone—man or woman—with a contemplative's heart will be.

These two perspectives, the material and the spiritual, represent the Yin and Yang of nearly everyone's interior dialogue. And certainly represents mine.

Definitions

In these chapters the friends examine:

- why the elders I call "engaged" develop their productive attitudes early in life—for instance, as they handle obstacles or conceive of aging in the first place;
- why authentic involvements produce a hopeful, ageless vitality and hope; and

- why fulfilling, transpersonal activities promote the will to endure and to grow beyond the common losses, pains, or seeming frailties of advanced age.

That last point makes this book relevant to readers of every age, given the continuity factor in what is now called *successful aging*: well-being, independence, or healthy autonomy, finding the right fit between ourselves and our environment, retaining control over life and its affairs. And more. If in later life we hope to be productive, joyful, and connected to others, if we dream about being optimally self-expressive, then we'll need to age "successfully" along spiritual lines.

I define *spiritual* as the animation of our core, essential self. The spiritual is our very breath of life—the quickening brought about by insight, understanding, heightened awareness of the transcendent. Spiritual awakening includes the good stewardship of one's soul. While I do not confuse the word *spiritual* with religion—creed; dogma; theology—there may be overlaps. Our fingerprint of self, the spark of life, colors our perspective, thereby shaping our convictions about the sacred.

Background and Biases

Those who wonder why I care about this topic deserve to know that I've had a lifelong love affair with human talent of every conceivable sort. Specifically I've spent my professional life mentoring and educating what psychologists term the "self-actualizing"—those among us who pursue and even embody their highest values, creativity, and worldview—their sacred "I Am." Even in childhood.

I began my professional career in the late sixties, serving first as a public school teacher—in the primary grades no less—then transitioning through the upper grades of teaching and the ranks of various administrative posts. In 1980 I left the public sector to start my own corporate development firm. My specialty was human resource and leadership development for both profit and nonprofit sectors. The upshot is that I've designed optimal learning environments for learners of every age—from kindergarten to Ph.D.-level students; from senior leaders of Fortune 500 companies to, most recently, mixed constituents of gerontologists and health-care and marketing teams in the life-care industry. For well over thirty years, I've been immersed in the strategic identification, education, and design of programs that cultivate people's functional excellence—their innate capability. Business and writing have only expanded my educator role.

All that has convinced me that much of what we

observe as decline in "old" age results from impover-
ished education. We *learn* our boredoms, our apathies,
and our regressive responses to the world around us. We
readily observe these programmed attitudes in our own
dysfunctions, in those of family life and the work environment, on which I have been focused for years. Unad-
dressed, our symptoms of *learned* helplessness or lack of
mental stimulation may simply increase with age. By
contrast, those who live robustly into later life cultivate
a real vocation—purposes or pastimes they love. They
develop intimate, trusted relationships. They possess
that sturdy moral compass that theologian Paul Tillich
called "the courage to be."[4]

Our acceptance of ageist biases are the product of
*mis*education. We should assess the cost of ignoring our
false beliefs. These false assumptions depress vitality,
interests, and loving participation with others. False assumptions thwart our "courage to be," turn existence
into banal life-scripts, largely conceived and controlled
by others: the mass media, our social set, or those we
consider authority figures (like doctors, social service
agents, or even our children). We swallow hook, line, and
sinker whatever sad fictions about old age we've been
taught. For instance, that later life is necessarily a sickly,
lonely, alienated time. Or, that as we age, we aren't able

to learn new skills. Or make new friends. Or have new adventures. Or contribute to others. Or live independently. Research suggests otherwise, as the following dialogue of encouragement explains. However, research comes and research goes. Time and again, "facts" prove to be fiction. The earth is not flat. Humans can walk on the moon. Diseases like polio can be eradicated. Change is constant. Only the Spirit remains the same yesterday, today, and tomorrow. To center ourselves in the Spirit— to awaken spiritually—is to endure. We forget this. We look back wistfully to the good old days, thinking the best is gone for good.

From the beginning of time, dreams of youth and "the good old days" have mesmerized humankind. And still today, we chase youth. Who can blame us? Life is sweet.

Yet, our sweetest life, our truest life, is with us always— beyond the senses, ever rooted in consciousness. Generic experience reveals what we know down deep. Dreams, near-death, and peak experiences; shared values about the sanctity of life, family, or home; the universal refreshment we all gain by truly encountering, really seeing, a crimson sunrise or a shooting star—all such reverence, all such awe, testifies to one brilliant Reality. Just a glimpse, just one recollection, sparks joy. Rich or poor, young and old,

almost all of us sense something sacred in the invisible—
something eternal that outlasts earthly life. At our ground
of being, we are ageless, never "old." However, we are, in
varying degrees, only just awakening to this eternal fact.
And yesterday's prophets knew better, knew enough of
the Everlasting to drink deeply from its well. So it was that
Solomon with all his wisdom could sing,

> . . . for now the winter is past. . . .
> The flowers appear on the earth;
> the time of singing has come,
> and the voice of the turtledove
> is heard in our land. . . .
> Arise my love, my fair one,
> and come away.[5]

I

The First Exchange

~ On feeling old and useless ~

*The sufferer must be urged onward
in spite of himself . . . and when he realizes
that he can put himself again in connection
with the world and fulfill [worthy] tasks,
a being he did not dream of before
unfolds itself within.*

Helen Keller*

---

*Helen Keller, *My Religion* (New York: Doubleday [Swedenborg Foundation], 1972 ed.), p. 145. (Paraphrase is mine.)

"My Little Aches . . . Loom Large Today"

Dear El,

Here I sit in wistful reflection. It's raining. Dark clouds and a chilling wind hint of a cold, harsh winter fast approaching. Yes, dear friend, you grasp my drift. I speak of more than just the weather.

I'm in the dumps. Feeling old. Useless, if you must know. My little aches and pains loom large today— "badder," much more ominous than ever. I ask myself, "When did this turn occur?" Is it hormonal?

Unlike this time one year ago, when my oh-so-important job kept me busy and the kids lived closer, now I'm twiddling my thumbs. Used to be that my Day-Timer was so jam-packed with appointments that I knew what I'd be doing for months ahead of time. Today, not only don't I have enough to do, but I'm clueless as to next steps. I want to do the "right thing" with the rest of my life (Remember: Next Spring, I'll turn sixty-eight.), if only a right move, in any direction, would present itself. I've been meditating on that Thomas Merton prayer you once sent me—the one on the little gray card with a verse from his *Thoughts in Solitude*:

> I do not see the road ahead of me. I cannot know for certain where it will end. Nor do I really know myself, and the fact that I think that I am following your will, Lord, does not mean that I am actually doing so. . . .[6]

Or, something like that. Anyway, that's where I am. My future seems cloudy. I don't *feel* old, but people have begun to treat me oddly, and I'm responding in kind.

Remember the law of reciprocity?

If people smile at you, you'll smile back. That's the interpersonal rule—a little like the self-fulfilling prophecy theory: If teachers believe their students are dull, why then the little darlings perform dullwittedly. Conversely, if other teachers think the very same students are bright, they'll learn smartly. Reality follows our assumptions. Did you tell me that?

Lately, my assumptions are riddled with ageism. Perhaps that's why, on planes, young flight attendants call me "dear." Have I somehow projected my feelings of decline onto others who then become patronizing? Or do they adopt that ultrafamiliar tone simply because my hair is white?

Then there's my son, Robert. He's warming up to odd new themes—inquiring about my will, asking me to sign some sort of power of attorney paper, hinting that he'd like to control my business affairs. Fat chance. And may it never be. The great news is that he and his wife are expecting a baby. I'm thrilled. Still, each new grandchild moves me one step closer to doting old grannyhood, one step further away from my corporate role. Instead of leading troops, I'm changing diapers.

Bear with me: one more whine.

The firm I *thought* would offer me that CEO's post has changed its mind. So here I lounge, reviewing my options, uncertain, watching time fly by and—horrors of horrors—actually flipping through the glossy pages of those slick retirement-village brochures that my daughter keeps sending.

Everything around me, even my little cat, Moo, seems to be crying, "You're washed up. Outdated. Irrelevant." In response, though I stroke Moo's white furry head, I grow anxious.

Like clothes out of season, my good old days seem packed away for good. Where has the excitement gone? I miss my executive authority. I miss the work I've loved, the team spirit of building up a business, that mindless chattering at meetings where, all spruced up in Armani suits, I celebrated wins and losses with peers and planned for rosy futures. I miss those airless flights to bustling cities, those revved-up conferences that got me inspired. How strange: That harried, thankless schedule held my life's purpose. Today, my choices seem fear-based and wishy-washy. Forgive me, dear, I'm in a self-pitying mood. To paraphrase the old folk-song, it's only a worried man who sings a worried song.

Before I end, one question: You've written much about self-actualizing children and adults. Well, what happens to such types in later life? Send me a glad word on them. Or anything. Quickly. If anyone can cheer me up, you can. Well, gotta go. It's time for my mood pills.

Love, Bo

To me, fair friend, you never can be old,

For as you were when first your eye I eyed,

Such seems your beauty still.

William Shakespeare*

*Sonnet 104.

21

"Let's Become an
Encouragement Team"

Hi Sweetie,

Got your letter and not to worry. For all such heart-
aches Julian of Norwich sends a message: "All will be
well . . . you shall see that every kind of thing will
be well."[7]

I have a hot idea—a project, if you will. But first, a
news flash: I empathize. Oh sure, in dog years I'm
younger. But slim Lolitas already call me "dear" in inso-
lent tones. Not so subtle, either. As you point out, all of
society—advertisers and marketers especially, it would
appear—conspire against the aging individual to snuff
out that wholesome confidence that breeds self-respect
and direction. You can't turn on the TV without images
of gray-haired people popping pills or rubbing linament

on their sore joints. When I'm a centenarian, and so rickety that no one dares retaliate, I'll poke the pointy tip of my umbrella into the ribs of any young one who uses That Tone. Let's accent the affirmative. Let's say "Yes" to life—adopt a new mind and self-renewing, productive expectations about advanced age. That means dropping the worn-out view that equates old age with hopelessness. Let's tell ourselves the good news, like . . .

"Just because you feel old, doesn't make it so!"

Indeed, our projections or assumptions cause problems. And, yes, I have said that. However, that principle about assumptions creating reality is a metaphysical law. Not original with me. It grew popular around the nineteen hundreds, and possibly earlier, as part of the New Thought revival. Philosophers of the day like Douglas Fawcett, Thomas Troward, and Neville Goddard embraced the Law of Assumption as the means whereby we fulfill all desires. According to Goddard,

Each assumption has its corresponding world. If you are truly observant, you will notice the power of your assumptions to change circumstances which appear wholly immutable.[8]

To keep our courage up, we must correct our patterns of thought. It's folly to lose our confidence at this critical juncture. Isn't advanced age (I won't say "old") exactly *the* time to dig down and dredge up a fighting spirit? By controlling our assumptions, we expand our happiness, live a nobler life, tap into the imperishable. I'm not talking about laminating cheery sayings over our feelings in an attempt to get happy, but actually turning our thoughts to God's Thoughts. As Isaiah remarked, these are higher than our thoughts and ways, and revolutionize our life.

There are so many ways to come at this! Metaphysics inquires into first principles, explains all in terms of consciousness. Mystics are the experiencers—ecstatics who attend exclusively to Eternity—not to their own "viewpoint about Eternity." They're "intuitive, not discursive," and consider intellectualized systems only *after* their raptures end.[9]

A beautiful prayer works wonders!

You know that my spirituality is of an intuitive nature. I'm no ascetic. Quite to the contrary, my very cells feel rich. That's especially true when I'm chewing on a verse of scripture—anytime, and particularly if I'm uneasy about something. The psalmist and the prophet

Isaiah uttered some of my favorite lines for such rumi-
nating. For instance, Isaiah promises,

> For you shall go out in joy,
> and be led back in peace;
> the mountains and the hills before you
> shall burst into song
> and all the trees of the field shall clap
>   their hands.[10]

In due time, as I ponder these words, they shift spontaneously. The verse becomes a transformative prayer
and tips my mind toward gratitude. I begin to appreciate
the natural world anew—breathe in the divine Love *as*
fresh air. See God as clouds, and, yes, hear self-existent
Life as the "trees of the field clapping their hands." Every
ant, each rock, fairly shimmers with divinity. Seeming
magic occurs when thought affirms the here and now.

Author John Cantwell-Kiley, M.D., writes that we
invite the "birds of sorrow to nest in our hair" when,
instead, we could so easily and at once let our own
thought patterns grow "a tissue" of healing over our
pain. To feel better, we need only to lift our thought—
expand awareness *beyond* anxiety:

You must realize that your mortal enemy is not your loss, but your *thought* about your loss. You must learn to defend yourself like an expert. . . . The trees and the sky through your window can fill your consciousness, in any moment you choose, with their quiet healing presence. The real world, in other words, will rescue you from grief, if you allow it to enter your consciousness.[11]

The trick is to cultivate that beautiful present-centeredness that invites insight and awe. Then there's action. As a friend used to say . . .

"The whole universe rejoices in my right action."

One of my favorite (old!) professor-therapists used to preach to us bright-eyed graduate students: "To change a mood, take an action in the *opposite* direction." He meant that to shift a blue mood to a sunny one, we must move—however slightly—in positive directions.

In an eye blink, one small constructive act improves our mentality, what author-metaphysician John Hargreaves, concentrating on consciousness, calls our "*altitude* of thought." He's writing *only* about thought. But for me, action—something simple like cleaning out the tool chest—lifts my spirit. Of course, thought begets action. I used to believe I lacked the mindset and physical strength for manual labor. Unhelpful assumption! Last week I refinished my deck. *Alone.* The improved view alters concrete reality for the better. That must be why scripture advises, "Let the weak say I am strong."[12]

Now here's an initial positive move: With your doc's OK of course, consider exercise. Run right out to find anything you can about senior athletes—for example, books about men and women of advanced age who run marathons or swim outdoors in January with the Polar Bears. They are amazing mentors. Their courage is well worth emulating. For them, advances in age seem like advances in hardiness—the dynamic purpose and sturdy character from which inner triumph flows. People in wheelchairs who play basketball reflect such courage, such strength. It's not their physical prowess but their *spiritual* hardiness that amazes me. By which I mean: *spiritual* as our "animating essence." And *hardiness* meaning, well, "hardy": potent, buoyant, indefatigable.

I own a photo compilation of vibrant, real-life warriors.[13] One seventy-two-year-old began jogging at age sixty-five, shortly after she retired. A decade later she was running five miles a day. And, dahling, she looked *fabulous.* Sitting here in Oinker Mode, scarfing up the last crumbs of a Sara Lee cheesecake, I see clearly now—that vitality is for me. The next time I reach for a big bag of greased-up munchies, I'm going to tell myself . . .

"I deserve to be fit—within and without."

Men and women of eighty, ninety, and centenarians can be fit, trim, and luminous. It's rarely too late. However, self-actualizing elders aren't necessarily fitness buffs. Could be. Do not *have* to be. (Ever see pictures of Stephen Hawking, the astral-physicist? Or, Eleanor Roosevelt? Or Helen Keller? They appear to have fitness of spirit.) "Fit" assumptions—now that's what I'm after. Which brings up your intuitive question about self-actualizing adults in later life.

"Awakening" as engagement and spiritual fitness.

You hit the bull's eye: If it's *spiritual* fitness we want, then self-actualizers are most assuredly the ones to watch. Young or old, they're ageless, inspiring guides to adding life to our years. I call older self-actualizing adults awakening when they are "engaged"—absorbed with something, anything, that truly delights. The full encounter lets the individual grow self-aware. Now consciousness knows itself, from within itself. Most of us admire such individuals. Thus the awakening are also attractive—magnetic; "enga*ging*." Not because they've had fat globs suctioned out of their thighs or hair plugs sewn into their balding skulls, but because they're busy discerning the meaning of life.

The self-actualizers are mostly ordinary men and women who extract extraordinary messages from the things others overlook. Whatever's happening—even little mundane events like a chat with the bus driver—they're growing from those experiences.

To illustrate: A distant neighbor is a counselor of some sort. He's well over seventy and totally blind—perhaps since birth. I don't know him, but it's my impression that he's always learning. He still works and lives independently. He resides alone, along a remote and rugged coast. Observing him at the market, or at the bank (on the days a college student accompanies him on what, apparently, is his errand run), he seems more self-sufficient, more cheerful and more fit since I first saw him—years ago. He actively serves himself and others from the gifts and circumstances that make him unique. I call him engaged—"gainfully employed" and fully occupied—because he encounters life robustly. He's turned on. He's grappling with experience, however it's dished up. Isn't that *our* goal? That's already the ambition of millions.

We inhabit an awakening planet.

Consider recent polls that report eight out of ten baby boomers plan to work at least part-time during retirement. More than 80 percent of those who have pondered their future say they feel optimistic about their later life.[14] Those numbers reflect a new collective consciousness, a raised awareness or a global awakening to the potentials of advanced age. To the extent we keep on learning, growing, and stay connected, old age isn't what it used to be.

Aging has changed because our human community is coming alive to the promise of life—all of life. Most of us expect to remain healthy, independent, and productive throughout life. The whole world stands at the brink of that new thought, that revived assumption about living well in later life and even dying with dignity.

Which brings up my red-hot notion: If you miss the team spirit of business, why don't *we* become a team? We're long-distance, but so what?

Let's become an encouragement team.

Our team purpose could be to give and receive mutual support, to further the hardiness or inner strength from which life meaning flows. We'll encourage each other to keep on keepin' on. And why not? Haven't we done that for eons, from afar, for business reasons? While not exactly a commercial venture, our exchange will fix our attention on the productive assumptions we want.

As mentioned, John Hargreaves is one of my favorite metaphysicians. He proposes that a change of consciousness is necessary for a change of evidence. In a universe of consciousness, what we think about ourselves and the world *becomes* our world.[15] What could be more glorious than to wake up to an eternal immutable existence, beyond our sense-world? It's not our carnal mind that's "awakening," but our spiritual depths. Why don't we share ideas that structure ageless vitality—that inner wealth? Let's realize . . .

"I am not my pain!"

If you're game, when I write next I'll say a bit more about that interior vitality or quickening. In that spiritual framework, what you're now experiencing could be a precursor to the first awakening step—that first dawning insight when, sick and tired of feeling sick and tired, a flash of comprehension reveals all is not what it appears to be. "Aha!" sighs Insight, "I'm not my body, not my pain, am so much more than this troubled circumstance." Who knows what might result from a dialogue on enlightening themes?

You've read the statistics. So many older adults *feel* useless, depressed or unattractive because they *believe* they're over the hill. The huddled masses believe they are powerless. Too often they are emotionally destitute. Those who age successfully are focused on meanings, intent on living with a kind of flair. I've known quiet, self-effacing poets and horticulturists determined to express some interior beauty. Then there are the more obvious leaders—the Margaret Thatchers, Madeleine Albrights, John Glenns, and Nelson Mandelas of our world—who capture our imagination in a big way. Not just because they're rich and famous, but because they reveal their values, their loves on a large stage. Solitary or social, such people give us hope. It's hopeful thought we want . . .

Hope flows from living love.

We need to plant seeds of optimism and self-power in our minds, especially in our later years. Hope is subjective—it's the *feeling* of God with us. Emily Dickinson's word on hope as a ceaseless "song" with feathers, perching in our soul, makes me say that with hope, we, like Solomon, can sing these boundless lines, "Behold the winter is past; the rain is over and gone. . . ."[16]

When your new grandchild stares up at you with round infant eyes, you'll feel that sort of hope welling up. That's Love stirring, awakening us to Itself. That awakening is our healer, our life-fuel, our spiritual power. Awakening spiritually, we'll feel that strengthening love.

Now is the hour to side with the Spirit . . .

Each added year we can grow inwardly stronger. This seems *the* task of aging successfully. Truly, I do not know how crass materialists age with a glad heart. However, I do know we need not be formally religious to enter into that spiritual feeling, what St. John of the Cross called the secret chamber of love. Surely that's transcultural. Muslims, Buddhists, Christians, and Jews, and I'd think agnostics, too, can feel bursting with spiritual ardor. Isn't it in life's winter that we most strongly yearn to understand the Afterlife? In plain English, spiritual awakening lets us side with the Spirit—not the "flesh"—when our body cries that we're too old, sick, or feeble to stroll about outdoors or travel to Paris with friends.

I'm not saying don't get that hip replaced or that chin lift. I'm saying "the flesh" is not *my* focus, not my area of interest at all. I side with St. Paul: Our outer self does seem to age, but alive in the divine love, we enter an ageless, immutable Reality.

Encouragement adds to vitality.

Eclectic educator that I am, executive exemplar that you are, can't we muster up the ideas by which to shape an enterprise of optimism? Our respective track records of achievement will produce continuity of skills, strengths and attributes for a better way of thinking. Most of us over, say, the age of sixty-five, seventy or eighty want *a way of being* that stimulates optimism. Who gains that without consciously rejecting all the hype about so-called old age? Both self-encouragement and supportive fellowship support such goals. What do you say? Shall we lift our minds above the fleshly paradigm of aging? Ironically, practices like yoga or tai chi stretch thought into those flexible new realms.

To get us started, here are questions for you: Can you send a few ideas on continuity theory and "successful aging"? For instance, what are the links between life experience and successful aging? I sense learning links here. Won't the sheer increase of retirees in society require quality attention—in the form of improved home care, health care, public policy, and related job counseling? You're the executive-development guru. What's your vision of the leadership implications for this era of global aging? How might corporations, communities, health-care professionals, and families encourage greater self-sufficiency and optimism in elders? It's malnourishment of mind, not body, we two should address. That's assuming you agree that in later life, it's the proper care and feeding of the soul that needs attention.

Finally, I close with seven words. My gift of cheer. The next time rude shop clerks call you "dear" in snobby, supercilious tones, or your kids send you "over-the-hill" messages, let them know it's not age that puts us over the hill, but the assumption of decline we ascribe to aging. Remind them that you're growing in a rare, spiritual direction. Then lay these seven little words on anyone who discounts you due to your years:

Don't call me old. Call me *awakening*.

Isn't it time we reclaimed and celebrated the wisdom, the sheer spiritual intelligence or inspired thought that comes with the years?

Love, El

P.S. To repeat my bias: Check with your doc to be sure, but how about taking jaunty, brisk walks at the beach? And afterward, maybe relax with some delectable Greek olives and a glass of chilled Chardonnay. (But just one, right?) And, before sleep at night, I say don't watch the news. Try watching the Marx brothers in some classic farce.

I love *The Simpsons*. A belly laugh, or several, before bed must be good for the soul. Let's not forget that the state of mind with which we enter each night's rest can either mobilize or degrade our very life force. Perhaps that's why parents, through the ages, have taught children to "count your blessings" before sleep.

Plus, speaking of enhanced care of the mind, how about munching on an uplifting statement—actually ingesting it, as you wash dishes or climb stairs? A line like "the joy of the LORD is your strength"[17] may be cryptic at first, but by chewing on such phrases in a deliberate way, you dive into your intuitive depths. So comes awakening—the quickening of higher consciousness that knows no limit.

II

The Second Exchange

*~ In which the friends explore
the self-leadership that overcomes
ageist assumptions ~*

*W*hen you get as old as we are,
you have to struggle to hang onto your
freedom, your independence. We have a lot
of family and friends keeping an eye on us,
but we try not to be dependent on any one
person. We try to pay people, even relatives,
for whatever they buy for us, and for
gasoline . . . things like that, so that
we do not feel beholden to them.

A. Elizabeth (Bessie) Delany,
age one hundred*

---

*Sarah L. Delany and A. Elizabeth Delany, with Amy Hill Hearth, *Having Our Say: The Delany Sisters' First 100 Years* (New York: Dell, 1993), p. 297.

"I May Join a Gym!"

﷯

Dear El,

You lifted my spirits to the skies. As for becoming a team, well—count me in. This is the spiritual companionship I crave—more substantive than merely social, and stirring, at the core. I'm all revved up—more jaunty walks and, with dinner, one (big) glass of hearty Pinot Noir. Yes, Yes. I checked with my doc, who says, "Good idea." So now, full speed ahead.

First, loose ends and random thoughts:

Your word on optimism brought back author-biologist Lionel Tiger's premise that the expectancy of favorable outcomes is one underpinning of longevity—in both individuals and groups. I love Tiger's line (and I'm paraphrasing) that although he doesn't know what drives young dancers to break their bones and drive their bodies to achieve such grace at each performance, it is certainly not pessimism.[18]

Next, considering the war between the Spirit and the flesh, one question sprang to mind: "If I didn't know how old I was, how old would I feel?" Honestly, if I wasn't always receiving negative, ageist feedback from the media, from impudent sales clerks, from my family— even from myself—I'd feel about thirty. This alone wraps a band of truth around the rule that "assumptions construct reality."

That metaphysical principle seems simply a variant of the William James theme, that if we believe life is worth living, our belief creates the fact. Moreover, it's good to be reminded that life's all about thought, beliefs, and consciousness creating reality. Some quibble about that word *belief*. They say pure knowing is what works. I rest my case on Jesus' promise that

All things can be done for the one who believes.[19]

Let's keep this simple.

More on that in a moment. It relates to leadership for a graying society. Before that, a caution: I'd hate to over-organize such topics. Government and institutions seem to be getting into the spirituality act. For any kind of awakening, give me a small group of friends to talk with; a rousing intimate discussion; one or two inspired teachers who walk their spiritual talk. As individuals, shouldn't we take greater responsibility for *self*-leadership, for control over our own lives? For instance, since your letter, I'm puzzling over new questions like . . .

- To what and to whom do I listen or give power about the issues of age?

Since we're all interconnected, whoever wakes up to their authentic purposes and power enables others along similar lines.

Hardiness relates to positive rebellion.

I see this now: I must teach others how to treat me. That takes time. Considering my grown children, I know I have work to do. And, wasn't there something sobering you told me once about a quality called "positive rebellion"? Please remind me of that. I lack the assertion—or aggression, or rudeness?—to defend myself when doctors, nurses, and shop clerks are demeaning. Isn't their arrogance a form of abuse? Years ago, Art Linkletter succinctly wrote that abuse of senior Americans takes on many disguises. Abuse happens in and out of nursing homes, and abusers come in every shape and size:

Consider the following: being called grandma, grandpa, dear, or other patronizing names; continual sarcastic or insulting remarks; being told what a burden you are.[20]

Linkletter reminds us to utilize the regional ombudsman services that exist expressly to help us cope with abuse if we need the help later in life. Love the idea. We're not all alone—even if, when trouble strikes, it feels like that.

Now here's my "take" on much abuse: To get treated properly, we must first treat ourselves well. Our "no" must mean no! We'll teach ourselves how *we* wish to be treated. We'll wake up to better, healthier possibilities. I want to imagine brighter, more intelligent contexts for my life. I want wisdom, the attribute that age enhances. For some reason, this task of awakening wisdom makes me anxious—it asks me to move out of my comfort zone.

Maggie Kuhn, founder of the Gray Panthers, was right: We older people are risk-takers. We often forget we're innovators. Just think of those who travel around the country in mobile homes, after spending decades at a desk or in one residence. They're actively developing new models for living. Kuhn herself jumped in to organize the Gray Panthers' intergenerational activism when she was already in her sixties or seventies. She took on tough causes.[21] She possessed wit and boldness. By contrast, here I sit. Inert. Some of the risks I've been avoiding involve my children. When did I become afraid of them?

If we've learned to speak up and handle day-to-day problems adroitly, we'll have a semblance of authority when family or friend invades our space. When competencies grow, as need arises—throughout life—then in later life, again as need arises, we'll have a rich reservoir of capabilities to draw from. Like wit!

A recent *Guideposts* story of an elderly man recovering from surgery at a hospital speaks to this issue. He was vigorous, "but still immobile, without almost complete assistance." One day, the nurse sat him on the commode, left him alone, and failed to return. He hit the call button. An hour later, there he still sat. Repeatedly, he hit the call button—without response. Then his own wit surfaced to rescue him. He crawled over to the phone, dialed 911 and gave the operator his location—room 730 at such and such hospital. "Soon all the nurses in the world were in his room."[22]

That's "positive rebellion" — life-supporting, self-assertion.

I'll wager that man's ingenuity found productive outlets earlier in life. Psychotherapist Rollo May said that wholesome spontaneity amounts to apprehending a complete "picture" of what's happening situationally. We respond "to a particular environment at a given moment."[23] Sounds like that old Zen Buddhist adage that, ideally, we should act as if our hair were on fire—without inordinate intellectualizing. In other words, our wit serves us as we serve the here-and-now, wittily.[24]

That's continuity in aging.

As I understand the continuity theorists, who and how we were when younger is who and how we'll be when older. If we develop our authority, we'll have it to use when some nurse ignores our call button. We just continue the life we've known earlier. Well, maybe yes. Maybe no.

Many older people who graduate from the stresses of family or working life cross over a critical threshold of change. They get a wake-up call. They realize, "Life is passing by. I'd best get on with my original dreams of what could be." Then they up and tackle whatever's calling. It's really never too late. One such woman remarked,

> For many years, making a living, raising a family, all the anxieties that go along with that—I didn't

think as much about spiritual life as I do now. Now it colors everything I do, everything I think [and read].[25]

The news contains stories of men and women who, upon reaching their ninetieth year (or in their forties), find out they have heart disease, and turn with newfound vigor to the deeper side of life. To me, *that's* spiritual awakening: We yearn to encounter life truthfully, to express our meaningful ambitions no matter what the cost.

When America was attacked by terrorists on "9/11," all our lives changed. After the shock, the grief, I thought, "Wow, if there are things I want to do, I'd best get on with it." Spirituality surfaces when least expected: At any age. How might the continuity folks address these awakenings?

Who was it that said if we've *evolved* we'll be spiritual? While the evolved are already awakening, the less evolved appear to wake up with traumas and losses, but the least evolved tend to experience such massive denial about aging and death they never awaken. It's grace that shocks us out of our complacency.

Small, incremental self-victories build staying power.

As we age, we tend to cultivate our creative gifts if we've set a productive pattern in motion earlier. The first—the peak experience, or "shock" of awakening, seems a grace. The second, a choice to honor our authentic delights, is a quality decision: We decide to be genuine, at each juncture, consciously follow through. That's just like it is in business.

Who arises on their ninetieth birthday with the inner dynamism of a Zen master if, before that, they've wasted their gifts? The spiritually hardy keep plugging away at their dreams.

Didn't Mary Baker Eddy establish the *Christian Science Monitor* when in her late eighties? And, didn't Mother Teresa—ailing with heart problems and long into her eighties—persist in her work with the dying in Calcutta's slums? She possessed a functional excellence that most younger people envy. And, isn't Eartha Kitt, in her seventies, still entertaining with gusto? And, newsman Mike Wallace, in his eighties, is still going strong. Many, if not the majority, of our U.S. Supreme Court justices are in their seventies and eighties and still flourishing[26]— because that's what they've always done, and probably always expected to do. Nothing ethereal here.

Speaking of which, did you know that hardiness has a firm foothold in the psychology of the workplace? An eight-year study of 259 midlevel executives during the thirty-year breakup of Illinois Bell proved that it was not *absence* of adversity that produced hardy executives during what's been called "the greatest reorganization in corporate history."[27] Rather, the character and coping mechanism of the hardiest executives buffered them against debilitating stress. Their assumptions—there's that word again—enabled what researchers called their "transformational" coping skills. That is, these executives believed that . . .

- they could control or influence the events taking place around them;
- they could pit themselves against the adversity, viewing it as a challenge; and
- they could commit to overcoming the very problems that others feared.

That's "engagement."

Feeling committed, in control, and challenged helped the effective managers devise solutions for situations that overwhelmed the low-hardiness workers. The latter exhibited the learned helplessness and intense stress of victims.[28]

Outgrowing that vulnerability is an educational challenge.

I'm not precisely equating advanced age with stress or infirmity. However, inevitable losses occur—the death of old friends, the sense of isolation, feeling devalued by a society that favors youth on every conceivable front. We need productive self-leadership—if only to get out and meet new people when it's scary or inconvenient, to seek companionship in spite of ourselves!

Take the Delany sisters—two reclusive, charming centenarians.

These amazing two showed enough independence and pluck to bolster anyone's optimism. They coped transformationally, with wit and courage, in a racist era. Bessie Delany became a dentist; Sadie a high school teacher. Each spoke her own mind, in her own fashion. The more assertive Bessie thought it was "her God-given duty to tell people the truth." Sadie countered with a different strategy saying, ". . . don't you realize people don't want to hear the truth?" Over time, Sadie grew more assertive, admitting, "Truth is, I've gotten so old I'm starting to get a little *bold*. . . ."[29]

Self-leadership involves lifelong learning.

In educating ourselves and others toward "awakening" or spiritual hardiness, don't you think intent is a key? As a case in point, Sadie Delany started yoga when in her sixties. Bessie turned eighty, felt that Sadie looked better than she did, so took up yoga, too. In their seventies and eighties, the two began eating more healthfully. As one described it, "as many as seven different vegetables a day. Plus lots of fresh fruits . . ." and vitamins, whole cloves of garlic and cod-liver oil each day.[30] It seems they decided to live long, and asserted their will in wholesome directions. They made purposeful changes as needed, throughout their lives. That's self-leadership. We influence our own destiny.

To manage a longer life we'll need self-influence skills—by which I mean our ability to rein in low tendencies—indulgences, timidity, and the like—and rouse increased health and integrity.

Don't you think public policy needs to acknowledge *model* programs—the best-case answers and "success solutions"? These prototypes pave the way for a leadership that goes out in front with answers (rather than crying about problems). Instead of lambasting us with unhappy statistics about the trials of old age, would-be leaders can encourage hardiness by

- providing models of "successful aging";
- supporting community retreat centers that teach the elderly new, revitalizing skills, like yoga or chanting or prayer;
- sponsoring small-group dialogue to further dialogues of encouragement, as we have.

Then there's vocation—your area of expertise. Of course that includes work. If 80 percent of us expect to work in old age, won't career counselors and human resource professionals have their hands full? Many elderly now work after retirement, but few corporations are prepared for what's coming. Work provides engagement: the more engaged we are, the healthier.

Society's challenge, it seems to me, includes all the areas we're discussing. We need to open up a national dialogue on such issues as . . .

- rediscovering one's delights after retirement.

People who stay excited about their involvements long into old age are still rare. If you're an ex-president, a U.S. Supreme Court justice, or a media star, you may not need encouragement. You'll have money, social contacts, and continuing clout. But the vast numbers of elderly who want to keep working could easily feel rejected, discounted, insecure. These notions of engagement might improve their capacity for self-renewal—their authority over circumstances, their confidence. How do we, as a society, encourage greater aliveness and dynamic purpose? Since our only limits are the ones we accept in our minds, what success-models can we locate?

Please applaud my diligence . . .

I've found one spiritual exercise that plugs me right into the here-and-now. It's practical. Comes from a book of Tibetan meditations that build "mindfulness"— the high, clear awareness that diffuses negativity and turbulent emotions:

> Rather than suppressing emotions or indulging in them . . . [view your] thoughts and whatever arises with an acceptance and generosity that are as open and spacious as possible. . . .[31]

I know you prefer contemplative prayer, but this observational method works best for me. I'm learning. First thing in the morning, I sit quietly at my window with a cup of hot tea to warm my hands. I just "watch" my thoughts, viewing each one as if it's a scene in a movie. I'm kind to whatever mental pictures arise. Perhaps you'd call this a forgiveness exercise, since I'm "accepting" my mental state. I note the destructive, worrisome thoughts in order to extinguish these, eventually. (I'd call it a "know-thyself" exercise since "forgiveness" sounds too goody-goody for me.) Anyway, after observing my thoughts for a few minutes, I get on with normal routines. Later, if some unpleasant thought grabs my attention, I try to greet it with "an acceptance and generosity that are as open and spacious as possible." So far, so good.

Plenty of food for thought here. Or drink, as the case may be. While signing off, I raise my glass of Napa Red to you. Ah yes, only one glass, but large and tasty to the very last drop. Try this wine with a soft, ripe Brie and black rye bread. Too good. As for walks in fresh air, unlike you, I long for chatter when exercising. I may join a gym. Better yet, know anything about personal trainers? And one day soon, do share more about the "stages" of spiritual awakening. Seems a mighty fuzzy concept to me!

Cheers from the Brie-and-wine brigade, Bo

P.S. What have you heard about feng shui? You know, the ancient Chinese art of interior and architectural arrangement? Ha! I see you grinning irreverently. But really, I hear—when done correctly—it promotes success and well-being.

The religious geniuses of all ages
have been distinguished by [a cosmic
religious feeling] which knows no dogma
and no God conceived in man's image. . . .
Hence it is precisely among the heretics
of every age that we find [individuals]
who were filled with the highest
kind of religious feeling. . . .

Albert Einstein*

---

*Albert Einstein, *The World As I See It*, Alan Harris, trans. (Secaucus, N.J.: Citadel Press, 1979), p. 26.

"I Say, 'Hire the Monks'"

Dear B,

Bravo. Your ideas on self-leadership are pure gold. And your observational practice sounds lovely. Definitely a "know-thyself" practice. And so gentle. Too often, our human solutions involve force—what we can do; what we *will* for ourselves. We put our faith in the stock market or in our corporate connections.

As for spiritual companions:

The rare, beautiful words of Abishiktananda—that French monk who lived in India—best sum up this relationship: Our spiritual friend is God, who comes to meet us in the form of this or that human brother and sister. Through our love and respect and "humble service" we encourage both self-and-other to draw out the potential for divine life, which exists in the depth of the Spirit.[32]

One reason I prefer contemplative prayer to the repetition of cheery affirmations is that contemplatives often meditate on scripture. That becomes a prayer of the heart. Because it encodes the law of love in our consciousness, scripture invites God's *action* in us. It is creatively potent. Our mind recognizes something of itself, "sees" its true nature, in the Word. God's Word *is* the living Presence of divine love. That structures the spiritual universe that we yearn to inhabit. For the very "worlds are framed by the word of God."[33]

Spiritual awakening is progressive.

As for your question about stages of spiritual awakening: Some believe there are three phases to awakening. Others, like mystic author Evelyn Underhill, put it at five: First, comes insight: We sense, "Hey, there's more to me than this banker's job or my chronological age." Next comes purification: Now we take action to demonstrate our higher perspective. We tell our meddling relatives to mind their own business. Or, we accept life's next challenge, whether it's veering away from a nine-to-five job or ceasing our pointless gossiping. It may feel scary, but as understanding grows we consciously clean up our act. These first stages of awakening often come in spurts—can be dramatic. We feel shaken up. Our old viewpoint turns on its head. Later, as spiritual under-standing deepens, it is subtly nuanced, bringing forth a new way of life.

For instance, illumination, the third "phase," comes as our sense that God—the divine love—is closer to us than our breath. Mystics tend to feel this phase as a brand new life. Christians view it as the birth of the second Adam, the "new man" coming alive within, com-municated, as Thomas Merton often wrote, as the Holy Spirit draws us into the Risen Christ. We *hear* evidence of such experiences in the ecstatic tone of, say, poets whose verses swoon about love, lover, desire, or bliss. We *see* evidence of that encounter in the renunciations of the saintly who, despite some sacrifice or vows of poverty, feel rich beyond measure. Illumination is most vivid on a deep, subjective level—it's consciousness that's "awakening," purifying, no matter what else the outward appearance seems to indicate.

Surrender, the fourth stage, develops as we realize that, of ourselves, we can do nothing. This "dark night" has us betwixt and between, as it were: Although we've moved beyond the early delights of our meditations or insight, we feel far from God. We know there's much more in life for us to do, but feel stuck. Now strong faith becomes critical. Like E.T., we're far from home, temporarily in an alien land, obediently awaiting further instructions!

Finally, comes "union" with the divine Love—what Underhill called "the end toward which all the oscillations of consciousness have tended." Here is the peace, the sense of completion that lets us feel, "I now drink freely of the water of life."[34] Most of us don't move beyond the initial stages of awakening, simply because we want to swallow a magic pill of enlightenment, want to *feel* better instantly—without delays or effort.

Small choices advance integrity.

So first things first. To wake up spiritually, we must turn consciously toward that stillness that is a holy Presence. Rightly disposed, our five minutes of meditative stillness evolves into tranquility. At our core, we'll feel grounded. That's the healing—wholeness—we really want, no matter what else is happening. As you say, it is a discipline. However, the smallest choice can further that growth.

A friend says that most of us believe, erroneously, that to grow spiritually we must do something showy—don white robes, publicly donate vast sums of money to the poor. But, she insists, "In the spiritual life, small, humble gestures unleash vast reservoirs of unseen power. Look at Jesus. He took a towel, got a pan of water and began to wash his disciples' feet." To me this says if it's strength we want, our simplest act should "cleanse" our own— and others'—ground of being.

Such gestures are often spontaneous—the impulse of a cheerful giver, perhaps a giving known only to ourselves. Plus, if it's true that in later life we can become isolated, withdrawn or even self-serving, then an unobtrusive kindness toward another is not simply loving. It's restorative. Our own generosities lift us out of narrow concerns to wider, healthier relations. We're not giving to feel better about ourselves—not tithing or donating blood to get something in return—but contributing because our true name is Bountiful.

Keep the do-gooders away from my door!
Like you, my knee-jerk reaction to the mere mention of institutionalized spiritual support was, "Good grief, protect us." I side with whoever said, "Keep the do-gooders away!" And please don't get me started on exhibitionist, celebrity gurus.

Can those social scientists who lack reverence for God—or who haven't directly experienced the benefits of, say, prayer, meditation, and the contemplative arts—possibly illuminate our understanding of spirituality? Isn't traditional psychology an outgrowth of that legacy that promoted religion (and by association, spirituality) as the opiate of the masses? To study light, why consult anyone who's spent a lifetime in darkness? I say, along with Job, let's not follow those for whom "even the morning is as the shadow of death."[35]

I say, "Hire the Monks. . . . "

Why not retain monks, mystics and the cloistered as experts in matters spiritual? Those who have spent a lifetime praying in the Spirit could be ideal facilitators of spiritual dialogue. Openhearted dialogue is what I'm after. For instance, the *International Bulletin of Monastic Interreligious Dialogue* has reported for *years* on the articulate from all faiths who gather for trusting, two-way conversation about a shared transcendent reality. This isn't about dogma. It's about celebrating life. Imagine the uplift we might have if small groups of Buddhists, Muslims, Christians, *and* Jews *and* New Thought practitioners *and* poets and artists and others with a transcendent sense exchanged ideals, as we are doing. Interested retirement communities or life-care centers or institutions can host such gatherings. To infuse people our age with optimism, we'll have to open up that timeless spiritual window, "from whence heaven pours out blessings that there shall not be room enough to receive it."[36]

Now, to me, *that's* leadership. And it's also continuity: You're helping people create rituals that celebrate subtle, progressive advances in awareness. You're being present to one another—learning from those with deep feeling for, and a real experience of, ultimate Reality. That's not an intellectual concept. That's a concrete gift of leadership that could guide and facilitate processes such as . . .

- dialogue sessions (about timeless contemplative practices);
- spiritual journal workshops;
- meditation and prayer programs.

The possibilities fairly shimmer. Think of the harmony and grace that the elderly might experience if such programs were handled effectively.

Hardiness calls for inspired education.

In this, I rather love psychiatrist Thomas Szasz's word that, "You can't teach an old dog new tricks, but you can an old person. That's the difference between dogs and people."[37] We *can* learn, can awaken—at any age.

Continuity theory may ignore the Damascus experience. Wherever we are, we can be so struck by ultimate Reality that, for a time, we—like Saul who became Paul—cannot see through our old "eyes." That grace comes when least expected. No continuity there.

On the other hand, spiritual hardiness is as much a character issue as it is educational. *That* can be learned. We can understand and cultivate its virtues. And that learning is not born of increased physical strength but of courage—"the courage to move ahead *in spite of despair.*"[38] Although the word *hardy* can mean sturdy and strong, its inner dimension interests me. Endurance; robust intent, tenacity and, of course, courage are spiritual qualities that enhance daily life. Do share more of that industrial research in your next letter.

We're hardy at our ground of being.

Since my last letter, I've mulled over the animating nature of spiritual awakening. It relates to the living Love at our ground of being. For this, nothing informs me as richly as the lives of mystics, artists, and the saintly whose testimonies concretely reflect the illuminative turn of mind. Such people show us how to "see Light" and live as its reflection.

In *The View from Eighty*, author Malcolm Cowley

reflects that receptive, open mind. He believes the creative are among the most blessed and spiritually hardy. He is not extolling physical strength nor cosmetic beauty. He's describing people like Grandma Moses, the housewife from New York who "began painting in oils at seventy-eight, when she found her fingers were too arthritic to hold a needle." Then there's Renoir, who kept painting "and magnificently, for years after he was crippled by arthritis" with a brush strapped to one arm. And Goya who, at seventy-two retired to work "only for himself," and at seventy-eight was still working furiously, having escaped some uprising in Spain. According to Malcolm Cowley,

> Goya was deaf and his eyes were failing; in order to work he had to wear several pairs of spectacles, one over another, and then use a magnifying glass; but he was producing splendid work in a totally new style.[39]

Or, Giovanni Papini, a writer who kept writing although nearly blind, and who, upon being nearly incapacitated with muscular atrophy, then dictated his books. These artists are passionately engaged. Anyone whose love lets them work feverishly until the end, is—to me—an artist.

Our own engagements can lead us to such mystical spheres.

Cowley reinforces my bias: Our saints, our mystics and metaphysicians, our artists of every variety are living masters. Like Meister Eckhart or Hildegard of Bingen, they're often "heretics" who directly experience, then express the radiant consciousness of, say, prayer in its spiritual—not legalistic—depths. I don't mean that all such people pray formally. Just that their creative processes invite a boundless reality. Let's learn from those whose gainful employment expresses a divine ideal or an affirmation of life by which *we* would be guided.

Spiritual hardiness is a by-product of awakening.

True contemplatives and, of course, true artists are divinely intoxicated. Their hardiness flows from that—from drinking what, in her insightful story about Brother John of Parma, Underhill called "the cup of ecstasy": St. Francis offered the chalice of life to Brother John and the other brothers. John of Parma drank of the cup completely, devoutly, and without hesitation. And "straightaway he became all shining, like the sun." The others sipped tentatively of life's chalice, spilling much of it. As a result, they grew dark, misshapen, and miserable. Brother John alone was "resplendent above all the rest . . . [for he had] *more deeply gazed into the abyss of the infinite light divine.*"[40]

What is this "infinite Light" or cup of Life, if not the knowledge of God, the Transcendent? (For me, that's knowing Christ. Maybe for you that sentiment is over the top. However we phrase this living drink, it satisfies abundantly.)

Unlike John of Parma—and alas, too much like those more timid Franciscans in Underhill's story—most of us reject our drink of life. That's why we experience ups and downs, life as dual—part light, part dark; now this, now that. Wholeness of mind brings wholeness of experience.

Only the spiritual turns the seeming losses of aging into gain.

As you say, so much of later life involves children leaving home, friends passing away, the loss of hearing or physical stamina. If, to face such privations, we borrowed from the world's legacy of contemplation—what with its well-examined experience, its imagery of Dark Nights, its willing detachments or dyings to the small, "split" self—we'd gain a perfect framework for the incorruptible benefits of aging.

It's like the story of the guru who taught her disciples that liberation from loss comes when possessions affect our heart like a shadow of the bamboo tree on the court-yard.[41] We could learn that advanced age is a progression of understanding. It's not simply a piling up of chrono-logical years.

Can spiritual hardiness be learned?

Ultimately that liberty translates into compassion, en-durance, patience, the charitable acts of neighborliness. I confess this hardiness issue fascinates me because of its spiritual dynamic. We're fascinated by what we most need to learn. You know how I love comfort, how loudly I moan about petty annoyances—a hangnail, a paper cut or the lack of decent coffee in the morning if, say, I'm traveling. The way of holiness brings interior strength. Isn't the gaining of spiritual strength part of awakening?

How might we use those hardiness studies you've cited from industry to frame aging as a spiritual chal-lenge, rather than just a physical liability? Much like those disciplines stemming from the monastic—or if you prefer, the musician's—tradition, where "practice, practice, practice" cultivates proficiency, the traits of spiritual hardiness would let us commit to goals with overarching meaning. Or help us better tolerate those age-related losses you described. All we need for that is one powerful, divine idea.

Martha Wilcox, a Christian Scientist writing in the mid-1900s, proposed that once we accept a divine idea in consciousness, it "will unfold and bless and heal us throughout [the years]." The right or divine idea is a living, conscious, irresistible power that demonstrates itself and works the works of God.[42] We need leaders capable of understanding such themes—capable of initiating a new dialogue about possibilities.

As a youngster, I once had a salty, eighty-something pal. He hated hearing people's war stories about their surgeries or arthritis. He'd actually ask his poker buddies to leave his home if they rambled on too long about their aches and pains. Friends *loved* his company! I'd like to follow his lead, converse mostly about a valued future, or about books, music, and noble ideas. For starters, send me a teaching story about someone who's reinventing him- or herself in later life, redefining the idea of "old," living as if . . .

I'm not "old"—I am awakening.

If, as I've heard, leadership takes thought where it's found and lifts it higher, then those of us who call ourselves influencers should be helping everyone understand the beauty and logic of fresh, inspiring ideas—like Emerson's notion that

> Age sets its house in order, and finishes its works, which to every artist is a supreme pleasure.[43]

All Peace, El

P.S. Being an early-morning walker, I know less than nothing about personal trainers. Have you tried Pilates? Most enjoyable. You can do it at a gym (or at home). It's strengthening and relaxing, simultaneously.

Feng shui? (Heh, Heh. You're right. I *am* grinning.) Never tried it. I've heard it's an ancient, holistic system that integrates balance and nature into daily life. Scholarly experts now use it with multinationals and individuals before their corporate offices or homes are built. Something about intent—placing wind chimes, chairs, and entryways in correct "energy corners" and keeping red goldfish (live) on your desk in lovely bowls of water so that prosperity will flow your way. Hey—whatever gets you through the night, right? Seriously, here again, conscious intent and, more, the mind or assumption beneath the intent creates reality.

III

The Third Exchange

~ Concerning material versus
spiritual approaches to aging ~

We surround with respect
those old people who do not ask for it.
We ask advice of those old people
who do not insist on giving it.
The old have something better
to do — to become [our] confidants.

Paul Tournier*

*Paul Tournier, *Learn to Grow Old* (New York: Harper & Row; London: SCM Press, 1972), p. 19.

"Tell Me Only the Practical Stuff"

☙

Dear El,

Today, I'm devil's advocate. Some ethereal tone in your last missive concerns me. I understand your dedication to a contemplative life. Sorry, but you're in the minority.

The mainstream won't relate to your "saints-and-artists-have-it-best" theory. Personally, I get more excited by the thought of my new grandchild's birth than by your mystical notions. Yes, I want bright, healthy assumptions. But how do you answer the zillions of agnostics who say, "All well and good that metaphysical types grow closer to God with each passing year, but I'm not given to prayer or matters mystical"? Are you saying that destines me for decades of sorrow in my later years?

Too many older people are profoundly lonely. They're the ones I want to reach.

How about restating some of your spiritual biases in democratic terms that include everyone? For instance, all this chatter about "cups of Life" turns me off! Who experiences that? When you talk to your other friends about such topics, what approach succeeds? Stay on terra firma. Tell me only the practical stuff! As for your motto, I prefer to say, "Don't call me old—I'm just waking up. *Awakening* sounds so mushy.

All right. End of lecture.

About transformational coping, here's a story:

With your interest in corporate hardiness, I gladly tell you "Joe's" tale (not his real name). Joe is nearing retirement. Two years ago, Joe lost his job in a corporate reshuffle. He was in reasonably decent financial shape, but the displacement hit him like a Mack truck. Joe said he felt numb—inert—for a couple of weeks after hearing the news. He grieved. He grew confused. He feigned interest in the outplacement service that his firm provided. Finally, he got angry. Then he took charge.

Somehow Joe restructured his dilemma, framed it in learning terms. He said getting angry armed him, helped him feel alive and spot options. Ultimately he chose one thing over another:

Life's an adventure. We're put here to learn, to out-grow our helplessness.

My attitude took a hairpin turn the minute I remembered how much I enjoy solving problems. After all, that's been my livelihood: People pay me big bucks to apply my mind to business problems. So now I'm putting my mind to solutions on my own behalf—and it's fun. This disruption in my routine is teaching me so much.

Joe, who plans to exceed his former achievements, says, "I loved my old position, but today I want more control. Maybe I'll start my own business." The minute Joe reached beyond his problem to new levels of self-mastery, he started coping transformationally. This means he . . .

- interpreted adversity as a challenge (rather than a doomsday event);
- assumed and acted as if he could influence things for the better;
- dealt with the problem from an optimistic, active posture (rather than a victim's passive or pessi-mistic stance);
- put matters into a context of growth, learning, and advancement (rather than responding from an assumption of learned helplessness).

Joe chose to rise up and meet his challenge. He responds to stress with the transformational coping skills that recruiters seek out in their "hardy executives." By contrast, we cope "regressively"—ineffectively—when we avoid problems by drinking, overeating, or zoning out on drugs. Junk TV can distract us restfully for awhile, but over the long haul it's fruitless. According to researchers Kobasa and Maddi our backward step "does nothing to transform the stressful event."[44] Transformational coping bolsters hardiness because we actively choose to put our circumstances in perspective, believe our choices benefit us, if only in the long run.[45] The neat thing is that with these skills we influence events *and* grow more capable. This calls for determination, discipline.

Few of us automatically use our subjective life—emotions or intuition—productively. We get bogged down in nameless fears. Or sidestep our innate competence. Once again, as in youth so in age:

Doesn't an enriched spiritual life free up assertion?

You've told me that, in youth, you learned to protect your gifts and interests. Irish novelist Christy Brown; inspiring Helen Keller; American painter Janet Scudder; Gandhi—all were self-protective. They studied the seeming limits of their respective situations—physical handicaps in two cases, abject poverty in another, and, for Gandhi, the love of virtue, contemplation, and the peacemaker's disposition that caused him to be solitary and sometimes bossy. Before their teens, youngsters like these actively shelter the inborn talent.[46] To manage that, each learns to "choose and arrange" life. It's a concrete skill that includes organizing life according to an inner vision.[47]

I know adults who *only wish* they could choose and arrange their affairs "according to an inner vision." Wishing won't make it so. Can we isolate the superior assertion skills that some children spontaneously employ to help aging adults learn that, despite feeling vulnerable, they can speak up? When discounted or abused, conventional politeness may be inappropriate. My wealthy friends retain social secretaries and lawyers to guard their best interests and they use these supports even with close family members. The poor, the disenfranchised, or the alienated elderly may need education here. The plucky become mavericks.

You'll agree that most saints, successful entrepreneurs, and certainly artists put themselves "out there." If we have something to say or do in life, we'd better follow suit—develop a fiercely independent mind. You can't wish for this or that but then cancel yourself out with ambivalence. When gray hair or chronic back pain hints that we're no longer able, it takes passionate purpose to reinvent ourselves for new avenues of contribution. Isn't spiritual awakening also a forward psychic movement? Without that progress we'll look back to the past or envy the ambitions of the young. Our job is to be active way-showers—not pontificators.

How can we grow beyond learned helplessness in later life without support? Friendship support. Educational support. Here's where it helps to consider continuity. For instance, we can ask ourselves:

- Are we able and willing to envision and speak up for a desirable future?

Look at Georgia O'Keeffe.

In midlife, O'Keeffe began driving back and forth between her homes in New York and New Mexico. Alone. Neither cars nor highways were what they are now. Imagine her boldness. Some might call her "selfish" for leaving an ailing husband on the East Coast to trek out to the Southwest desert to live and paint in solitude. With deeper understanding, we'll grasp the initial, creative forces behind her move: her hypochondriacal—perhaps controlling husband, Alfred Stieglitz; his ill-concealed anger at Georgia's refusal to play the role of traditional wife and helpmate; his fear and possessive nature—"hurt and frightened because he was unable to fulfill the need that New Mexico met for his wife";[48] and, above all, O'Keeffe's genius talent—the inner force that would not be denied. In later years, Stieglitz reconciled himself to his wife's independence. He actually sent her back to the desert out of admiration for the paintings she sent him.

O'Keeffe aged well, and beautifully. You might say dynamic spiritual ideas propelled her forward. Her gifts were in full flourish, greater in age than in youth *because* of her assertion—because she knew what made her tick. Using your lexicon, she had a vocation, as biographer Laurie Lisle explains . . .

> Looking back, Georgia liked to say that she did what she wanted in life and it just worked out. . . . But that explanation, with the implication that she played a passive role, is too easy. Besides her abundant artistic gifts, her triumph as an artist demanded a clear-eyed, unconflicted will. "I've always known what I wanted and most people don't," she declared once.[49]

O'Keeffe is one of my ideals. (Have I just contradicted what I said before? I never said your bias didn't have merit.) She illustrates the universal need to handle conflict—to manage our so-called "selfish drives" with spiritual intelligence, not merely programmed responses. In O'Keeffe's case such drives were life-giving, life-extending. Honoring these sorts of impulses in ourselves, we affirm inborn gifts that cry for release. That's self-affirmation—our existential "Yes" to our own existence.

O'Keeffe's passion reminds me of that old story about the master who spent all her time at work. When her students asked her why she worked so hard, she replied, "The fulfillment that soothes comes only from the living Love, and my work *is* meditation—the crystal focus that leads to such love."[50]

It's the adjustment to safe little lives that kills so many of us prematurely. We die straight out from lack of intrinsic passion. Or, we expire some place deep within merely from knowing that our own fears undid us.

Don't most older people need assertion reminders?

As women assume more responsibility in the workplace, can they care for spouses, children and parents? Many still have that "don't-be-selfish" mindset. Something has to give. The victimized won't be *able* to speak up frankly for what's needed; won't set boundaries—financial or otherwise—won't protect their best interests.

It's an old story: Have women learned nothing in the last century? Older men have educational needs, too. A dear colleague, timid about reaching out to friends until he found out he had cancer, made up for lost time. During his chemotherapy, he joined discussion groups at church, abandoning his staid corporate associates in favor of a new, more vital crowd.

However, women do comprise the majority of family caregivers—about 72 percent. About a third of all seniors rely on daughters or daughters-in-law for support. A mere 12 percent expect a son to help.[51]

When a friend retired she had to stop contributing financially to an aging relative. She grew so despondent that, for a time, I thought she'd require medical help. Fortunately — and get this! — her ex-husband talked sense into her and helped her set boundaries with her family. Imagine her economic plight at eighty or ninety, if earlier—say, at age fifty or sixty—she hadn't voiced her caretaking limits. We've learned our false guilts. I'd guess each of us has distinct educational needs.

Baby boomers need assertiveness training, too.

New economic realities surround all baby boomers, as well as upcoming generations. Scientists are now doubling and *tripling* the life expectancy of worms and mice with new microscopic surgeries, genome maps, and anti-oxidant drugs. Can life extension for humans be far behind? But longer life creates new challenges. Like my friend, a growing number of baby boomers want and fully expect to support their aging parents. Unless they're affluent, they're dreaming. Most have children to rear and (more than likely) to put through college, and mortgages to pay off, and their own retirement needs to settle. So many financial considerations. And there's the press of their own finest gifts.

Let's get real about caregiving.

Human and financial resources for elder care will drop in the next decades. The number of elderly who will require help is skyrocketing.[52] The future of our aging, huddled masses is at stake, given what we in the United States laughingly call health care. That's why I want to bring this entire discussion down to earth.

Early on in our exchange, you suggested we find productive models or prototypes. Well, former senator Bob Dole fits that bill. Paraphrasing recent remarks I heard on the *Today* show, Dole basically redefined the phrase "old age." His idea—and his example—is that "old" isn't what it used to be:

I thought when you reached 40, 45, you were mid-dle-aged—now I [agree] with a third of the popu-lation who, at 70, consider themselves middle-aged. Senator Thurman is 98 or 99—he'd probably be a senior citizen, but I'm 76, and I don't consider myself old. I'm growing older, but I take care of myself—I've lost my prostate, and one kidney, and part of my colon, but I'm healthy.[53]

Dr. Mike Magee, senior medical advisor for Pfizer, echoed Dole as he outlined findings from Pfizer's "Pulse Study." Exploring the day-to-day habits of senior Olympic athletes to determine what, if anything, they did to enhance their quality of life the researchers found the majority . . .

- stayed current;
- stayed connected;
- stayed in control.

Conversely, smoking, drinking, lack of exercise, poor interpersonal relationships, and economic deprivation make us old before our time. And depressed.

In my opinion, Dole is much like my friend Joe—a transformational coper. He's apparently developed a hardiness that's proven to contribute to a high-quality life. Many more elders will relate to someone like Dole than to, say, John of Parma or St. Francis or even O'Keeffe. To me, Dole, Kuhn, and O'Keeffe approach age spiritually—with their courage and faith up front. And they're practical. Pragmatic. I can identify.

Lest I leave you feeling that I'm unsupportive of your spiritual awakening ideas, know that I'm only saying, "Let's not leave the majority out of our equation."

I heartily agree that commitment adds meaning to longevity and engagements enhance life. Tepid won't do. Author Norman Cousins wrote that the tragedy of most lives is not death, but what dies within us while we're still alive. He called boredom the most costly disease in America. Deadness of spirit, not cancer or coronaries, shortens the life of both individual and society.

Yoga? I'm sold. Pilates? I'll buy that, too. However, for tonight it's my easy chair and a Beaujolais. And "soy burgers." Well, more like ground-round patties bolstered with soy powder. (I fix these for my aunts. I tell 'em, "Even if your arteries clog, you'll avoid hot flashes!") While munching—and sipping—I shall mull over this matter of healthy passion in later life to see what activities might boost that.

In peace, B

P.S. Meet Homer and Marge, my new red (well, glisteningly orange) goldfish. My sweet cat Moo is spellbound. And I feel richer already. OK, so this is not exactly contemplative. But give it a rest. I feel better, so please don't knock it! While watching H and M swim around, I repeat a couple of author Leonard Orr's affirmations: *"I deserve to be wealthy and prosperous, and life now rewards me with abundance."*[54]

The greatest measure of love
will not be attained by trying to
force the individual to give up his nature . . .
the greatest measure of love will be
attained when each one realizes
that love, the special love,
that is within. . . .

Goethe*

*Albert Schweitzer, *Goethe: Four Studies*, translated by Charles R. Joy (Boston: Beacon Press, 1953), p. 99.

"My Dear, the Huddled Masses Will Relate"

Dear B,

Fine. Call me chastened. (Not the first time.)

Can we simply agree that spiritual hardiness unfolds by degrees? That we look around for inspiration, and then—somehow, if motivated—we develop what's necessary? From heroic (what I'll call saintly) amounts to more moderate gradations, we adopt the attributes we value or require. We are born to become more and more of who we are, at our best. Isn't that an egalitarian process?

I only suggest that saintly men and women and, yes—even children as "old souls," particularly of the mystic or artistic variety—reflect a plucky genuineness. They are what psychologist Abraham Maslow called "peakers": people who easily experience transcendence. They have a primary process creativity marked by flashes of intuitive clarity. A *Newsweek* article suggests half of us are neurologically "wired" for such episodes. Such experiences help us love our neighbors as ourselves. Or, as Blake put it, we see Eternity in a grain of sand.

The mystical encounter fuels outer potency.

Furthermore, almost anything can trigger that illuminated state. A man wrote to me saying he'd had an out-of-body moment while walking through a museum and was never again the same.[55] Then there's the corporate friend who participated in a wilderness trek. Afterward, her intuitive clarity skyrocketed. So did her self-esteem. She felt she could surmount all the obstacles that had previously blocked her way. Fear and lethargy diminished. She started her own consulting business. I think she returned to grad school. The skeptic, the spiritually immature, believes such instances cause withdrawal, excessive interiority; *either* we are transcenders *or* we are powerful in the world. Hogwash!

To your "Let's be democratic about this," I say many of us—yours truly included—feel something akin to rapture when viewing a Picasso, listening to Carlos Santana,

Gerry Mulligan or a Bach concerto, or riding the Colorado rapids. A Henry Moore sculpture, a nightingale's trill can open us up to the glory of our interior landscape. So many of us are receptive to that beauty.

Maslow went so far as to propose the world was divided into two classes of people, "peakers" and "non-peakers." He believed that the more highly evolved among us are more open, have more peak experiences and, further, that "these experiences seem to be more profound . . ." and produce what we might call the "most fully human" people—creative; caring; humorous; joyful.[56] Despite such outcomes (and this next bit you'll love) "peakers" tend to be run-of-the-mill. They live "what we could call an ordinary life." They shop. They eat. They go to the dentist. They think of money, and they meditate "profoundly over a choice between black shoes or brown shoes, going to silly movies, reading ephemeral literature."[57]

When a character on a popular TV show woke up from a near-death experience, his nurse exclaimed, "You look as if you've just seen God." The stunned patient replied, "I feel as though I've just *been* God.[58] If only fleetingly, most of us have had a glimmering cosmic encounter. My dear, the huddled masses *will* identify. They can relate!

People are closer than you imagine to what's been called the innocent eye of, say, their feelings of awe, gratitude or—ouch!—boundless bliss (to coin a mystic's phrase). In the aftermath of tragedy, the overriding emotion everywhere—amongst rich and poor, of each locale—is compassion. We care deeply for one another. This is life's great secret. The world's scriptures have lasted because Planet Earth is inhabited with spiritual, not earthbound, beings.

However, I'll grant you this: we do need down-to-earth reminders of that openhearted receptivity, that "Aha!" experience. So, to your question "What works?" when I speak of such matters to friends, I'm honestly not sure. Usually, first, I hit a wall. I notice blank stares. Then I improvise—change my approach. It's an intuitive dance. I'll search for a *practical* rule of thumb.

Study available "success" models.

One positive, *democratic* action is to find and observe elders—of every variety—who seem to us well integrated, hardy, effective, or if you prefer, just "happy." For instance, centenarians are said to be at ease in their own skins. Your mention of Dole, Georgia O'Keeffe, Maggie Kuhn, and that Pfizer study suggests that you do this sort of study-ing naturally and that most of us have success models right in our family, our circle of colleagues and our community.

Observation is so helpful to healthy growth; so integral to how we've learned most everything else—to skip and waltz and use cutlery—and archetypes are learning ideals, not so much persons or personalities as an embodiment, an energy pattern, a pure "type" or developmental aim.

We need not meet face to face or be spoon-fed by our mentors to benefit from their way of being. We can simply pay attention to what they *are*—to their being and doing—and heed the values they reflect. There's a spiritual ideal behind every virtuous archetype or mentor: The able executive reflects intelligence and leadership; the healer embodies a broad compassion. Our desire for wholeness (holiness, if you'll permit me) prompts our looking around for such spiritual ideals. And, yes, I see that advancement toward wholeness, or full integration, *is* actually "grounded in the stuff of youth."[59]

Our search for healing patterns begins early.

Many of us chase after our ideal of wholeness with fervor. Our attention is like a heat-seeking missile. We notice everything: billboard signs, ad slogans, a stranger's chance remarks. The adage, "all roads lead to Rome" applies: Anything, even the sight of a little green tree frog, can animate our reverence for life—and fuel spiritual awakening.

Even without religious sentiment, we'll feel, "My heart is after something." We're like that seeker who's examining portraits of venerable Masters at a museum. He asks the guide, "Where are today's Masters?" Whereupon the guide cries, "Seeker! Where are You?!"[60] Just so, we hunt for the inspirations that will stir us from within. Our search for unity involves these images. Let's not kid ourselves: our quest for unity is spiritual—no matter how secular our vocabulary.

Back to the amazing Georgia O'Keeffe.

As one of the few women to carve out a solitary, productive niche while serving her own creative gifts, O'Keeffe was aggressive—not merely assertive. Even in girlhood, she knew what she wanted, what she was all about. But her life's motif seems saintly in its devotion, its single-mindedness. She was uncompromising. Established boundaries. Enforced them strictly. Chose and arranged her life. It's often said that we are what we do with our attention. O'Keeffe managed her attention with the vigilance of a drill sergeant.

Earlier you asked "how" we improve our mental set. I say discern an archetype's significance. Your archetypes apparently contain leadership motifs, given Bob Dole's and Maggie Kuhn's achievements of widespread influence. So many others fit that profile—for me, that includes women like Madeleine Albright, Barbara and Laura Bush, and Barbara Jordan. I mean, such lists run on and on. Then there are the leaders' leaders—like Billy Graham. Or, Nelson Mandela, who didn't really get rolling until midlife, after being released from prison. Or Dorothy Day.

Yikes, I'm loathe to say it: To me, Day, Graham, and Mandela are saintly, too. And why stop there? Our heroes and heroines are everywhere. Talent expressed at midlife and beyond is stunning—breathtakingly obvious. Every community has its fair share. Look at those who amazed us during the 2001 terrorist attack on America. "Ordinary" people rose to sublime heights of leadership—on the street, on airplanes, right before our eyes. They proved Albert Einstein's notion that "the example of great and pure characters is the only thing that can produce fine ideas and noble deeds."[61] We look at their example, and many of us change for the better.

Admire the living march of talent.

Depending on our ideologies and interests, what about emulating the virtues of a Muhammad Ali? Talk about spiritual hardiness! Or Albert Einstein or Peanuts' "father," Charles Schulz, or Mahalia Jackson or Bob Dylan? Or Julia Child or John Glenn? What about Bishop Desmond Tutu or the Dalai Lama? There's an endless, living march of inspiration from which to learn our brand of engagement, our life's motifs and purposes. Such lists should center on vitality, not politics. You say you're nearing The Big Seven-o. Well, sweetie pie, your regard for Dole, Kuhn, and O'Keeffe suggests your "leader within" is restless for some greater expression, perhaps some wider social influence.

Admiration fans the imagination, and the power of your imagination quickens passionate purpose. Your ideal condition will appear outwardly in direct proportion to your awakening to ideas.

Admittedly, my life's ideals include Jesus of Nazareth and contemplatives such as St. Francis and Thomas Merton and artist-educators like Ben Shahn. For me, these are leaders of a decidedly rarer breed than, say, the social activist genre. There's meaning here. Psychoanalyst Carl Jung proposed that the archetype is "rich in secret life, which seeks to add itself to our own individual life in order to make it whole."[62] Our self-inquiry must be this: What distinctive messages do our elder archetypes convey? Unless we get a handle on *why* we admire—or would emulate—this or that idea, value or virtue, we're likely to overlook the "secret life" that our archetypes hold and would add to our own lives.

Here's where journal writing, talks with supportive friends or therapy with some qualified, trusted counselor becomes relevant. Discernment is infinitely progressive. There's no end to growth.

How do we motivate the unmotivated?

Don't forget that I'm a card-carrying contemplative. I like to live and let live, not police anyone's thought processes. You asked, "What do you tell people who can't relate to this 'engaged elder' bit?" I say, "Let each one phrase fulfillment in terms each one prefers, and then just get on with the sublime purposes of life." If someone doesn't like my viewpoint, I say "Find alternatives. Change the channel." It's that simple. There's only one way to light a fire under the lethargic or inconsolable: *Encourage their highest awareness.* In essence, isn't that what education and competent therapy strive for? Paraphrasing Seneca, it's with our mind that we first travel from Earth to the stars.

If reality follows thought, belief, assumptions, then for the dispirited whose conventional ideas of aging sap spiritual strength, reeducation is in order. Have we convinced ourselves that, after age sixty-five or ninety, life is over? Do we repeat mantras like, "At my age, I can't afford to take such risks . . . ," or "I'm too old to make new friends"? If so, then with each passing year we hem ourselves into ever smaller cells of mind, thus limiting our options. When former president George Bush went sky diving on one of his milestone birthdays, he proved we're rarely "too old" to try something new—unless we think we are.

Leaders encourage an ageless engagement.

Now it's your turn. Answer me this: At what age does it become OK to *ignore* our inner summons to live connectedly, or to cut ourselves off from whatever we deem worthwhile? Aren't we, as older beings, also "advancing"—especially when we possess all our faculties? Aren't we responsible to live nobly, to *continue* learning, to keep growing in patience or wisdom or compassion? No, I am not saying that those who are frail should be obligated to work for pay or even do their housekeeping! I'm saying let's reach out to new odysseys of mind, to new friendships—at every age. Even that Pulse Study you cited indicates connections of all sorts keep us young on the inside, where it counts.

You can't *force* connectedness on anyone. Yet I've observed a few octogenarians motivate others by sparking new love of life in them. One ninety-something friend is a livewire with Parkinson's. His influence knows no bounds. Leaders like that possess productive assumptions. They work daily to rise above negative mental states—the self-thwarting suggestion. Author, psychologist Champion Teutsch describes that productive mentality as an ageless consciousness. He says we project our concepts, known or not, into our environment, and that projected mind shapes our universe:

> The environment is that part of yourself which you know as "me." Consequently, the projected self changes from moment to moment. It reflects your consciousness.[63]

Motivating leaders *live* in a constructive mental climate, eventually drawing others into their high atmosphere of confidence, their excellence. In effect, such leaders say to us, "You're important to this effort. Help us reach this new goal!"

Leadership pundit John W. Gardner explains such influence: In a free society, how we do our job—whatever it is—builds up, or lowers, the tone of the entire society, "And the man who does a slovenly job—whether he is a janitor or a judge, a surgeon or a technician—lowers the tone of society."[64]

His words are spiritual. If each of us does our little bit—writing, sculpting, dancing, or speaking our contributions—we'll teach by living example, thereby raising the level of individual optimism all the way around. In fact, this is what's happening: The majority of us feel as if life is worth living when we're contributing to others. I read somewhere that if only 5 percent of the over-sixty-five group would volunteer some time, that would result in over fifty million hours of contribution each week!

To paraphrase your challenge: Who in the world experiences Eternity?, forgive me, but I suspect most all the saints. And poets like Rumi, Blake, and Dickinson. And artists and musicians. And so many more everyday folks than we admit. That's why contemplative practices are so glorious: They help us know ourselves as we are, and were before the beginning.

A living legacy of sages can guide us . . .

Historically, Native Americans used words to reflect their reverence for issues we've only begun to explore. One Native American elder defined the word *sovereignty* in a fresh way, without leaning on one overripe buzz word:

Personally, I'm sovereign. I'm not dependent on anybody. For thirty years, I was a high-steel construction worker, and I loved it. It satisfied something in my ego and my manhood. . . . Then I had to learn how to make my family sovereign, how to make my people sovereign. Sovereignty is something that goes in ever-widening circles, beginning with yourself. . . . Sovereignty isn't something someone else gives you. . . . It's a responsibility you carry inside yourself.[65]

Isn't that what our exchange is all about? Aren't we building sovereignty? That autonomous or independent spirit begins with us and affects ever-widening circles.

Universality is key.

You said it: Let's find some common element, use a friendly dialect, invite everyone to our new-assumptions party. The language is close at hand. I'll sleep on it. So rest easy: I agree 100 percent—we shall democratize this discussion so that no one feels left out. Not even quaint little minority types, like yours truly!

Regards to Homer, Marge, and Moo
from Yours Truly

P.S. Meat-soy patties? Well . . . sounds healthy, but I'd prefer eggplant burritos. Here's my recipe, such as it is. Pare the skin off fresh, firm eggplant(s) and slice into patty-sized rounds. Brush with olive oil, "bread," and season to taste with garlic, salt, and pepper. Slice and sauté the eggplant in a nonstick fry pan (or grill) until translucent and well-cooked (but not mushy). Add chopped, fresh parsley and more garlic, if you wish, toward the end of your cooking. (I grill other veggies along with the eggplant—red peppers, zucchini, and sliced red onions) and place all that on a flat, ready-to-steam burrito wrap. Top with cheese (optional, natch), roll up, and steam. Enjoy with whatever condiments you'd usually use on regular burgers. I use a knife and fork (could be runny) and usually substitute a couple of eggplant rounds for one meat patty. Accompany this with a glass of chilled white wine, and you're all set. Yum.

As for me, I'm joining friends for a Charlie Chan marathon. (Charlie's going to solve crimes in Paris, London, and New York!) So, tonight, it's mushroom pizza and German beer. And the "flesh" shall enjoy itself mightily.

IV

The Fourth Exchange

*~ On living well, and living long,
and dying with dignity ~*

. . . And when your
children's children think themselves alone
in the field, the store, the shop,
upon the highway or in the silence of
the pathless woods, they will not be alone. . . .
At night when the streets of your cities and
villages are silent and you think them deserted,
they will throng with the returning hosts
that once filled and still love this beautiful
land . . . deal kindly with my people, for the
dead are not powerless. . . . Dead, did I say?
There is no death, only a change of worlds!

Chief Seattle, 1855*

*Chief Seattle, in Steve Wall and Harvey Arden, *Wisdomkeepers: Meetings with Native American Spiritual Elders* (Hillsboro, Ore.: Beyond Words Publishing, 1990), p. 125.

"Baby Boomers Are Redefining 'Old Age'"

❦

Dear Friend El,

Let's talk baby boomers. That's the huge "bulge" in the U.S. population born between 1946 and 1964. There are zillions of them. (Or, seventy-six million to be more precise.) The oldest are nearing retirement; most will do so before 2010.

Baby boomers are redefining "old age" and retirement as they go. They identify with the spiritual issues we're discussing: They're healthy. Hopeful. Confident and pragmatic. This crowd changes anything it dislikes.

Politicians, marketing gurus, and health-care agencies that don't get this will be toast. History. Finito. Count on it: In years to come, matters related to aging and end-of-life care will improve since baby boomers seem fully occupied with the idea of "the good life": living long and healthfully and dying with dignity and a sense of peace. Observing how their parents fare in old age, they see much to improve. Two friends I'll call Agnes and Matt epitomize the uprising that's taking place within the minds and hearts of baby boomers.

Agnes watched her mother live out her last years in a nursing home. It was the least objectionable setup that the family could arrange, the best of various unappealing options. The nursing home was a decent place. Nonetheless, it reinforced Agnes's determination to live independently throughout her own old age. She's not alone. A fear of losing independence is chief among baby boomers' concerns.

Then there's Matt. He represents scores of baby boomers who plan to alter the state of dying in America—if only for themselves. Matt witnessed his father die slowly, helplessly, and in pain—repeatedly resuscitated against his explicit (*written*) instructions. Matt wanted to respect his dad's wishes, but his brothers fought against it. The ordeal tore that family apart and cemented Matt's intent to handle his own death differently. It isn't death per se that frightens Matt but the thought of a lingering, vegetative demise. As he explained over a cup of coffee:

Those months that my dad was dying, he couldn't communicate. Watching his silent tribulation, I fancied him enraged at losing control over his own death after a robust, enterprising life.

Somewhere deep inside, I vowed to conclude my own life differently. Of course, there are no guarantees. But with any luck, I'll have advanced directives settled long before they're needed.

Don't you think our system is archaic?

According to *Time*, "1 out of 10 dying Americans said in a survey that his wishes (against over-treatment) were ignored."[66] Seven out of ten Americans say they wish to die at home. Sadly the majority still expire in some sort of medical institution. Imagine it: Over half of us die in pain, in unfamiliar beds, with strangers as caregivers in attendance. People want a "kinder, gentler death," but they aren't getting it.

Until recently, medical schools had not developed curriculums on managing pain or end-of-life care. Even now, a *third* of the clergy have had "no training to help dying people."[67] Worse: As individuals, many of us fear death, live in denial, and won't even mention the word.

The spouse of an artist I know warns him "not to discuss such morbid topics." Then there's the attorney who urged me to make out a trust of some sort. I inquired what features she'd used in her own trust. She admitted she hadn't created one yet. Furthermore, that seventy-something lawyer said she didn't have a will and "didn't want to think about dying."

Similarly, we may refuse to share our preferences for end-of-life care with loved ones. Over half of us have prepared "advanced directives" (i.e., legal, "living wills") that spell out our wishes for treatment. The majority of us never divulge our intent to anyone, not even our doctors. If we do prepare advanced written directives, only about 6 percent of us work with a physician to develop these, and

> . . . although many Americans legally designate someone else to make medical decisions after they are unable to, 30% of those who have been designated don't even know they have been picked.[68]

If we "live and let live," why can't we, one day, let go?

Despite the growing consumer demand for a dignified passing, my entrepreneurial mind fancies that we don't have a "kinder, gentler" death because dying is a profitable enterprise. The end-game of life brings big bucks to someone: Perhaps not to compassionate doctors, nurses, or those truly called to the healing arts. But surely *revenue* matters to some bottom-liners.

Time estimates that if you die in a hospital, you'll spend $1,000 per day, and in a nursing home, $1,000 per week. Compare that to the $100 a day for hospice care.[69] The word *hospice* comes from the Latin *hospitium*, or guest house. It's a term originally applied to places of shelter "for weary and sick travelers returning from religious pilgrimages."

Hospice is rooted in our right to refuse treatment, and "the constitutional right to privacy that includes determining what happens to our bodies."[70] With hospice care, death is gradually becoming a conscious blending of "God's will" and our surrender to it.

Like Matt, I expect to determine my own way of surrendering to the inevitable. Isn't courage to let go—to make that call—a critical component of spiritual hardiness? If you're offended by that question, let's just agree to disagree. (But consider this: Even selling one's lifelong home—tossing out old letters, giving away nostalgic keepsakes—takes guts. I went through that and, frankly, that letting go was a death of sorts, a grieving time.)

I've heard about aboriginal tribes whose belief systems

supported letting go of life when an elder was ready. East-
ern gurus, or adepts, frequently predict their own passing. They call it "dropping the body." I sense illumined
Westerners want consciously to adopt that state of awareness through the ideas and mental means that let them
relinquish earthly life when they feel the summons of
their next level of experience. There's another topic that's
ripe for the spiritual companionship we're sharing. You
will swoon over a little gem of a book in which two distant
pals encourage one another from afar. They're focused
on spiritual growth, not aging. Yet their mutual support
sounds like ours. One friend writes,

> . . . one important outgrowth of a dialogue like
> ours [is that] each uplifts the other while turning
> one's own mind progressively to that incorrupt-
> ible, greater life, [and] speaks so as to advance the
> other's true life in Christ.[71]

What a practical, admirable example of how friends can
lovingly draw forth the best from each other. These loving relationships empower us greatly during losses, and,
yes, during despair.

Speaking of admirable examples, when Jacqueline
Kennedy Onassis died, her son JFK, Jr., remarked that
she had passed on in her own way—with her loved ones

near, fully aware of the choices she was making along the way.

At each passage, including death, trusted friends can help one another, thereby growing in intimacy and loving trust. Assuming events cooperate, there are significant requirements for a dignified passing. At the very least, one needs inward strength; firm, perhaps heroic, intent. Let's clarify our wishes. Write them down. *Communicate* these to appropriate others—long before we get ill or hospitalized. As for me, I want to know *now* which family member will support my program.

Then, too, get ready for your own sweet time!

A great malaise can overtake us when we've loved our work and find all our industry, our hustle and bustle, our narrow pursuits at an end—when we are, as it were, "let out to pasture." Much midlife despair flows from our own lopsidedness, our false beliefs that life is over just because we're older. I speak from experience.

Back when we originally started this conversation, each day seemed pointless. Too much free time. My overscheduled world of work, bill paying, car pools, e-mails, faxes, and family life had not prepared me for leisure.

We're poorly prepared for unstructured time. Long before we reach life's second half, shouldn't we break through our constricted, overfocused career path? Swiss psychologist and physician Paul Tournier's reasoning is so solid:

> You my forty- and fifty-year-old readers, you have had to specialize narrowly to build up the fruitful life you lead today. You have had to give up many things which might have interested you. You have worked hard. . . . You have been disciplined enough not to spend too much time on (pleasure and relaxation). . . . And success has even further en- slaved you to your career. It is not enough for you to complain that you no longer have time for any- thing else. Consider what is at stake: it is to make sure that your life will be able to expand once more.[72]

Any expansion in later life comes from genuine pur- poses, poetry of soul, the true calling of whatever we love.

"To catch a fish, think like a fish!"

Baby boomers may look to their spiritual elders for inspiration, but mostly, they're reinventing retirement. They're feeling their way along—returning to college, forging new businesses, scaling mountains in Tibet, signing up to be astronauts or marathon runners at age seventy and eighty. They're pioneers.

Physically fit, late-middle-agers (both men and women) appear much like thirty-six-year-olds. They wear sneakers, faded jeans and designer tee shirts. Many older men sport ponytails. They stud their earlobes with diamonds. They ride souped-up motorcycles with their wives enjoying the road or hanging on for dear life. Women at forty, fifty, and beyond are bearing their first children. Today's middle-agers think young. That's why they're capturing the radiant aging experience they seek.

Just to be clear: I'm not chasing youth, just the ability to experience what Rollo May called *openness*: readiness to grow; flexibility; a change for the sake of enhanced values, and above all avoiding rigidity of dogma.[73]

Egads! I'm starting to sound like you.

Passionate engagement flows from authentic purposes.

The engaged or spiritually awakening elder will cast out the myths of aging, as authors Dr. John Rowe and Professor Robert Kahn explain in their book *Successful Aging*. They refute outdated stereotypes. Among other things, they've shown that the majority of elders are independent and continue learning and stay involved with others.

In other words: it's never too late to learn, to get (and stay) involved with doing what we love, and to preserve our independence. To achieve that involvement, however, I'm learning not to look back or try to revive old glories, and to move on much as if I were graduating from one plane of study to another.

Not everyone must be consumed by a great talent or vision or genius-level project. One can feel deeply fulfilled by hearth, home, and family pastimes. Positive attention—that's Love, isn't it? The healing, transforming factor. So we find things that we love to do, things we look forward to.

Every successful salesman knows that when the "have tos" become "want tos" miracles happen. If you love to bowl, you'll get up at dawn to join your league. If you hate bowling you'll pull the covers up over your head and sleep in. I heard about a single parent, on a budget, who'd made all her children's clothes from scratch using her old, faithful Singer sewing machine. After "retiring" she followed an impulse to collect antiques. Today, her cottage is a veritable sewing-machine museum—overloaded with time-worn, functioning Singers.

A neighbor in his eighties has become a master woodcarver, selling tiny little bowls for several hundred dollars each. Another retiree joined hospice as a volunteer. She tells me she's never felt more fulfilled. A collector of exquisite Asian porcelain began buying antique translucent china as a schoolboy. After fifty or sixty years, he's still patiently—lovingly—buying, cataloging, and preserving these precious artifacts. The only limit to such engagements dwells in our minds. If we *think* we can create an engaged life, we can! Which brings up my own imperatives.

When I first confided in you, my internal fires seemed dead. To no avail, I kept asking myself, "What's worth doing? What kind of legacy do I want to leave? What sorts of activities give me a lift—something to look forward to?" I was lonely. Old friends had either moved away or passed on. I believed nothing remained that could ever enchant me again. Our exchange jump-started my energy. I wanted that old spark, and got it. Answers have come!

Reconnecting with potency . . .

To begin with, I asked myself, "what's worth doing?" I began listing all the projects that I'd like to tackle with some seriousness in the next ten years. Check out my top three tasks:

- Take my grandchild on a tour of Ireland (my mother's birthplace).

- Organize an annual reunion weekend with my best friends from business.
- Revisit my life's "journey" through the assorted photographs in my old family albums, annotating benchmarks and noting the values, lessons learned, and the meaning of key friendships. (I'd like to make three copies of this photo-diary to give to my son and his wife, to my daughter, and one to my grand-child.)

I'm already immersed in that photographic journal project—feeling more energized and hopeful with each cut and paste. How surprising to realize that others fig-ure so prominently in my joy.

As for archetypes, I've also pondered my inner "ideal." Indeed, that meditation—if that's what it is—stirred up long-forgotten goals. Suddenly insight struck: What I need, what I want, is to build something participative by which to serve others, while exercising my leadership muscles. You've devoted yourself to teaching, writing, and a reflective artist's life. Business has always been my art—a fantastic team sport; my commitments are always fueled by cooperative projects.

Finally this morning, after a strong espresso, an epiphany: I shall create a highly responsive, interactive, service business related to much that we've explored—

largely to foster "awakening" in older people—to help them adopt productive, life-affirming assumptions. I hope to tell us all: "Reach out! Make new friends. Encourage one another by living well." I'm a skillful networker, and the relationships alone should serve everyone concerned. Hopefully, I'll know more in my next letter.

More on assertion and the coping that transforms . . .

The mere thought of starting something new fills me with zest. Could I have been depressed? Psychologists have long believed that it's women who are either more prone to suffer from depression or more likely to seek help for it (and are therefore labeled as "depressed" by health-care professionals). This *ignores* the obvious: Men also get depressed.

However, a study of 1,100 adults between ages twenty-five and seventy-five, found that "women may more often than men get caught in a *cycle of despair and passivity*" when there's a mix of (a) low sense of control over important areas of life and (b) more chronic strain and (c) a high degree of passive thinking about feelings. Those who thought more about their problems (and responded more passively) failed to do what they could "to overcome stressful situations such as an unfulfilling marriage or an inequitable distribution of labor at home. . . ."[74] The women in the study, more so than the men, apparently believed in their misery or felt deserving of mistreatment. Constant torment can do that to anyone, man or woman.

The psychologists conducting the study proposed two solutions:

1. Help women gain a greater sense of control over their situations.
2. Help them become more engaged in problem solving (rather than just thinking about it).

I say alert everyone—regardless of age or gender—to their learned helplessness. Help them untangle the hurtful regressive responses that thwart hardiness. Part of the good life is becoming an *active* solution finder, feeling in control of and challenged by problems. Trouble gives us a chance to grow, understand, develop our mind's muscles. Didn't Abraham Lincoln say he wasn't so much worried about getting God on his side as trying to put himself on God's side? To me that means aligning ourselves with the highest thought possible.

We merge with what we notice . . .

This bit about thoughts creating reality is sinking in. So I'm now chanting Emile Coue's classic affirmation, *"Every day, in every way, I am getting better and better."* As noted, that's not contemplative prayer—not the receptive, interior listening you prefer. For me—and I'd guess for most people—it's energizing nonetheless.

Generally, positive statements help us to expect positive things. These trigger mental images of goals. And stimulate the good vibrations that attract our good. Metaphysician Florence Scovel Shinn advised us to "make friends" with what we desire. That triggers the Law of Attraction that gives us such a sense of ownership over our goals that we'll draw our desires to ourselves. She says we combine with whatever we notice.[75] So now I am noticing my strengths, my blessings, and all the beauty around me. Truly, life is good.

Signed,

Getting Much Better, B

P.S. Charlie Chan? Well, thanks but no thanks. I realize you adore old black and white films, but really . . . spare me. (I am rolling my eyes in disbelief.) For uproarious fun, I suggest you spend time with the Brits on BBC-America. My favorite programs are *Two Fat Ladies* (or some such title! They are jolly, odd-duck chefs who slather lard and butter on nearly everything and make me want to do likewise!), *Monty Python*, and *Antiques Roadshow* (with all those endearing, eccentric, gray-haired appraisers). And, if you crave mysteries, try *Murder Most English*. Too charming for words.

Homer (maybe it's Marge) looks a tad less "rosy" today. Shades of goldfish death, I fear. Is there some inverse feng shui phenomenon happening? If Homer floats, will my stock portfolio sink? Where are the venerable experts when you need 'em?

Death is not a reality,
but the absence of a reality. . . .
But there is nothing lost
that God cannot find again.
Nothing dead that cannot live again
in the presence of His spirit.

Thomas Merton*

*Thomas Merton, *The New Man* (New York: Farrar, Straus and Giroux, 1961), p. 242.

"We Can Awaken from This Life to a Greater One"

🏅

Dear B,

When my remarkable neighbor, "Reggie"—widowed and childless—discovered she had inoperable cancer, she chose to die at home. She simply refused chemotherapy. She planned for the inevitable all alone, living out her last days in her own cozy, spotless bedroom. The space resembled a cloister in a fairy tale. Light poured in from beveled panes of French doors that opened on a sun-drenched patio. Reggie's irises were in full-bloom, blanketing the ground outside her room like a violet carpet. Tall pines bordered the garden, their green boughs bent low with quilts of moss. That little courtyard foreshadowed Paradise. No, I'm not romanticizing this:

Sitting there, all those days and hours, gazing out her windows, surrounded by earthly beauty, Reggie was preparing—saying her good-byes to this world.

A nurse lived with Reggie. Hospice volunteers came and went. Her gumption led me to revise my well-worn notions about dying. That dignity you mentioned—it never dies. So I agree: it would be a great service to help others meet "death" with some semblance of acceptance. However, for me, that meeting starts long, long before we face the end.

You alluded to that when describing your grief upon selling your home. There is a way of life that lets go, that dies small deaths as required, that vanquishes death by embracing a greater life.[76] It's a full-time job. Perhaps we demonstrate that through our mindful way of being. Or through small courageous acts. Certainly through forgiveness, kindness, charity, and simple, everyday integrity. Reggie taught me to accept whatever comes. Her yielding speaks to your plea to "let go." Only after reaching a certain point in consciousness, can we know, in and with Christ, that we pass from death into life.[77]

Look at Elisha.

It does seem possible to be translated out of this life. It's a grace, not an entitlement. Elisha's passage into the

Kingdom came with forewarning and a sort of trembling of his very ground of being. Along the way to that phase of awakening, some of us do know when it's time to take our bows.

For instance, both of my grandmothers died in their sleep. So did two favorite aunts (well, in fact, my only aunts). But there must be more to passing on. Why, I've wondered, must anyone develop a catastrophic illness in order to exit this scene? What's the point *unless* we're still learning (or teaching) something—something big—something vital that we'll "take" with us to our next plane of existence. Surely this must be so for those who pass on, say, in war—without warning. Or who heroically give their lives for others. Or who employ their pain as a cross, that they might reflect only the divine Light. It's my sense that the spiritually evolved die with a vastly different heart posture—whatever the scenario—than those who are grossly attached to the physical plane.

St. Clare, it is said, when she was dying, prayed, *"Thank you, my God, for having created me."* And St. Francis, when he was dying, was carried through the local towns and villages on the way to his final resting place, but asked to stop that he might say one final prayer for his beloved town of Assisi:

May God bless you, holy town, so that many souls are saved by you. May many servants of God dwell in you, and may many of your inhabitants be chosen to enter the kingdom of eternal life.[78]

I agree with Thomas Merton that, to the spiritually awake, ". . . all other lights contain the infinite light," that as we awaken to God as "the self" (neither some misty concept nor the Great Piggy Bank sitting judgmentally atop puffy white clouds), we meet the divine love as our exquisitely ageless Center, the breath of our being, the "imminent source of our own identity and life."[79]

Merton eloquently described the spiritually evolved as living—and passing on—from a transfigured heart that knows God as intimately and deeply as "the self." They're not theorizing. They're vividly encountering the divine love, "the passage through non-being into being, the recovery of existence from non-existence, the resurrection of life out of death."[80] Grace, forgiveness, gratitude—this is how we awaken from this life to a greater one. Yes, life is unpredictable. We don't always have the luxury of preparing ourselves for the passage we call death. However, all can choose, each day, to honor life. Further, those with a deep spiritual perspective sense "death" is unreal. Only Life, in some fashion, is Reality.

In much more mainstream fashion Dr. Elisabeth Kübler-Ross's specialty of end-of-life care gives us a peerless look at acceptance within the process of dying. Kübler-Ross, too, speaks of letting go. For her acceptance is far from resignation. It doesn't mean we're close to death or that we want to die. As she explains,

> . . . acceptance is our feeling of victory, peace, serenity, and positive submission to things we cannot change. . . . Resignation is more a feeling of defeat, of bitterness, of what's the use, I'm tired of fighting. I would estimate that about 80% of our nursing-home patients are in a stage of resignation.[81]

If we fear dying . . .

Circumstances may cause us to be absent from the bedside of our mother, brother, or aunt at their passing. People carry such guilt about their loved ones dying "alone." Yet, if we know that, somewhere along with their preparatory grief, they—like JFK, Jr.'s mother, and grandmother Rose Kennedy, or my friend Reggie—have reached an accepting state, we can rest easy. We'll trust that, in their dying, they were never really alone—not if they let go in love. It is impossible to feel that acceptance—that love—without also feeling serene. That love may cause some people to swear that when loved ones or patients pass on they appear to see a light or sense a beloved companion guiding them. For me, it is enough to know—as Mary Ward, an English nun, said—that God, who lays on a burden, also carries it.

Reggie was serene. She was courageous. I'd say that mix of attributes delivered the awareness of how she wanted to pass on. Years before, she'd lost her daughter. Then her husband. She reconciled herself to those losses. Small pleasures comforted her—books, her garden, the dawn light and chirping birds, a friend or two, a bit of family. Reggie was not religious. In her own way, she was spiritual. Her spiritual side was grappling with life's Big Questions.

One day, I brought her a watercolor that she'd always loved. While I was propping it up on her window sill, Reggie suddenly asked, "Tell me how you conceive of heaven—you know, the afterlife." So I did. Using Jesus' promise that "the Kingdom of Heaven is within," I shared my direct experience of Eternity as a harmony of heart—our very existence, the ascent of consciousness to everlasting arms that undergird us.[82] She listened intently. In the end, Reggie didn't wish to talk. So we just sat together in the quiet.

And speaking of preparatory grief-work, given both our experiences and the testimony of so many others, I'd say "retirement" or "graduation" from a life's career involves a good deal of grief-work: loss, anger, letting go, acceptance, finding next steps.

Here's how I'd answer your question, "Did I ever really live my own life?"

Remember the movie *Moonstruck*? Cher's character gets engaged to the older brother of a baker with one hand. Then Cher and the young baker (played by Nicholas Cage) fall in love. He believes his brother caused the accident that robbed him of his hand and a former fiancée. Cher rejects that idea, insisting we're each responsible for ourselves. She says something like, "You have a wolf within, a wild or elemental nature that knew you were about to ensnare yourself in a loveless marriage. Rather than let you destroy your life, that untamed essence helped you gnaw off your own hand, thus freeing you from your deathly trap."

Isn't it possible that what you call "living for others"— marriage, having children, *and* entering business—*is* your life? That, at your intuitive core, you knew that only a big, option-rich life could fulfill your unique destiny; that you'd use a loving marriage, parenthood, and a leader's influence to learn whatever lessons life had for you? Maybe, like Cage's character, you only imagine that you weren't responsible for choosing a journey with such diverse elements. Our spiritual intelligence is untamed. It's the refiner's fire that shapes us. It's what we most need. We spoke earlier of purification. Well, many experiences purge us, prod us on beyond our counterfeit loves.[83] In my own life, that "purification" has come from delays, despair, desolation. I wait for answers, realizing the things that hold me captive must be overcome. Waiting is a teacher preparing me for next steps.

We're never too old for passion.

In her old age, Jungian psychologist and author Florida Scott-Maxwell's ardor surprised her. In her eighties she grew more alive—not less—and more aware of who she was, more fired up than ever, despite physical frailty. Late in life, she underwent a serious surgery. Her chief fear was that she might become an invalid, ". . . a burden . . . someone who could not die."[84] Scott-Maxwell needn't have worried. As she recuperated, her independence was reborn.

At first, she loathed the hospital rules. She detested each invasion of privacy. Her rage was healthy. When

Scott-Maxwell finally growled openly at the nurse who sat beside her as she bathed, she found her old self had returned. As she explained:

> I wanted to say [to the nurse who directed my every move], "Let me alone, I'll do it myself," and oh my relief when the dear woman laughed and said, "You're the kind that get well quickly. Some want everything done for them, just won't take themselves on at all."[85]

We're not all like her. Only prejudice says we're all alike. The elderly are as diverse as kindergartners. Even in advanced years, Scott-Maxwell was an intellectual livewire. As she was in delicate health, she conserved her strength. Spoke little. Enjoyed the silence. Pared down. Simplified life. For example, she gave up goal setting with some relief, saying it was a comfort to abandon a lifetime of effort. At a certain point, she felt herself past action, past decision, and ready for a spacious, elevating emptiness:

> One's conscience? Toss the fussy thing aside. Rest, rest. So much over, so much hopeless, some delight remaining . . . one has only one's soul as company.[86]

Her focus, now narrowed to the essentials of daily life, seemed spiritual. Scott-Maxwell was self-sufficient, living alone in her little flat until her death in her nineties. Ah, but not all of us follow her pattern. Awakening to who one is can happen either in the midst of paring back to basics, or forging ahead to new activities. Each one's awakening is unique.

Every community across the globe knows its robust centenarians. Consider if you will one Ludwig Magener (a mere ninety-three). Magener swam daily, married a younger wife, and was an artist who painted with zeal. At age ninety he won the National Masters swimming championships in all the events he entered (six freestyle and backstroke). And always enjoyed his life immensely.[87] Consider, too, author Robert S. Wood, who applied his metaphysical beliefs to his own successful aging. As you are doing, Woods experimented with positive affirmations, continuing until he was "brimming with good feeling. . . ." His goal was to revive youth's vigor in every cell. For that, he had to focus his mind: He resolved to "grow younger." He wrote, rewrote, and refined a paragraph that "embodied" his intent and stimulated feelings of "radiant health." After turning that paragraph into an affirmation, he seems to have willed his desire into being:

Now, at 70, I feel younger, more energetic, more vibrantly alive, more capable and energetic than I did at 60. I know the cells in my body listen and obey my desire and emotion.[88]

I could go on and on. Surely, you get the picture. We create our world in and with our mind. We shape experience with deliberateness and feeling, as author Thomas Troward once wrote, with the great forming power and movement of thought. All that to say, it's right and fitting that you focus on another gladdening venture, that you speak positive words, and imagine, with firm intention, doing what you love. Blake likened the Imagination to God's creative power: We should befriend our "Images of wonder" if we would arise from our "mortal graves." So blessings on your work. I'll envision it at its best— gilt-edged and helpful.

As lifestyles differ, so do passions.

I am the champion nester. Home is a spiritual idea; my sanctuary, my zone of calm and comfort. It's where I think, write, invent recipes—and enjoy friends, my garden, and life immensely. Whoever else loves home is in fabulous company.

Carl Sandburg wrote poetry throughout his eighties, at which time he also began to raise goats on his North Carolina farm. Even late in life, Agatha Christie traveled restlessly from one residence to another (of her eight homes). Her biographer Gwen Robyns comments that Christie spent so much of her life sitting and writing in her own chambers, that she "enjoyed moving and a change of scenery." Furthermore, Dame Agatha's "passion for houses stemmed from childhood and the hours spent playing with her doll house."[89] She conversed with her fictional characters while strolling about in her garden, as she herself described:

> I go walking up and down the garden with them talking to Miss Marple, the Vicar and so on. Perhaps Miss Marple is having difficulty in her garden and her broad beans have not come up properly that year. You can feel it all happening, and that's right.[90]

Homes, gardens, family—these "live on" tangibly. Reggie proved these sorts of pleasures renew us, somehow resurrect us and themselves. Apple orchards, herb gardens, bonsai collections, pet rabbits, golf weekends, and of course a life's work seem essential to the good life in old age. I overheard one gardener say that as she was tending the plants her ancestors seeded, so her children will tend to her plants. Noted psychoanalyst Erik Erickson believed that we avoid stagnation by confronting a developmental task he called *generativity—the concern for and the giving of one's self to the future.* For Erikson, that concern or care entails love for persons, *and* love for our created works. It also "assures for the mature ego the right to be needed," granting us the privilege to need the young.[91]

"Fall in love with your future" was George Burns's advice.

Whatever we look forward to can be vivifying, and particularly (and, I suspect, particularly *for* those whose joys have involved family) our children, grandchildren, and great-grandchildren.

Malcolm Cowley's interviews with octogenarians revealed that the most cheerful "had recently enjoyed a family celebration, usually a golden wedding." One man from Illinois told Cowley that he'd had such fun at the eightieth birthday party that his children and grandchildren gave him, he began looking forward to his eighty-fifth year.[92] Others—like you—who'd been in business all their lives continued their enterprises. And you told me about an elderly woman, at the brink of death, who consciously postponed that passage until her great-grandchild had been born. Just about anything we anticipate with pleasure can keep our heart pumping. With our spiritual eyes we see a lavish universe. We feel grateful. Only with carnal eyes do we gauge our loss. The Bottom Line? Find something wonderful to love.

Loving absorption with whatever matters most to us is *the* great healer. Everyone benefits from that engagement. Not everyone has giant talent or an impressive intellect like Christie, O'Keeffe, or Sandburg. And many people don't have a spouse or children, grandchildren, or great-grandchildren. So what? Never mind what we don't have.

If we could only commit to something with all the interest we can muster until that turns into a love of sorts, we'd tap into a pure regenerative force. The larger and more dynamic our love, the greater its regenerative power. It's inevitable that I'll return to this theme later: It is critical to "successful aging." According to metaphysician Agnes Larson, each of us needs to awaken to three spiritual understandings: God; self; work. And, she adds, the three are one, fully integrated whole.

Paring down, simplifying, delighting in the ordinary furthers that understanding. It's not enough to devise pointless events, however "happy." To be infused with dynamic, regenerative power we'll need magnetic, bound-less purposes—larger than our small selves. Granted, an eighty-fifth birthday party, a health spa weekend, or a Paris tour are fun—but they're finite. More to the point: Are these meaningful for us? Do these develop our awareness of God, self, and our purposeful calling? There are countless ways to achieve that: We plan. We reconfigure an earlier vision in new spiritual terms to meet the generativity requirements of concern for the future.

We can locate compelling goals before we retire.

Ever since I've known him, a business friend has taken two weeks off during the first part of January. He devotes that period to daydreaming about the year ahead. He then commits himself on paper to those objectives that motivate him. His business has profited from his practice. Upon retirement, he continued that habit—with the result that he's never bored. Each year produces fresh, exciting plans.

Then there's someone like Dr. Jane Goodall. Decades of field work with the Tanzania chimpanzees enabled Goodall to frame her compelling purposes in terms of the well-being of future generations. As we read in her memoir, through the Roots and Shoots program Goodall's "generativity" now empowers the individual.[93]

Our democratic "X-Factor" is "gainful employment." It has universal appeal.

In our heart of hearts, nearly all of us strive to do with life all that we know we can do. Oddly enough, it's that fullness of living that gives us the guts to let go when it's time. Having learned whatever we came to learn, we graduate from this earthly school. Someone who's "born" to be a parent and who lovingly, responsibly, raises three children is not going to jump up from their deathbed and shout, "Oh my God! I forgot to become a dentist!" Should we seriously fail to live up to the mark we ourselves have set, *that's* when we suffer.

When all is said and done . . .

What counts for so much is our sense that life's journey has helped us fulfill our spiritual destiny. In other words, vocation is our universal call to wholeness that, among other things, teaches us how to love, trust, forgive, and enjoy. Whether we're quilt makers, grocery clerks, or x-ray technicians, our vocations point us to a way of being that is loving in intent—integrated at its ground of being—so that we serve the greater good. We were born to learn that.

To people of all ages I say locate that avenue of functioning or unique way of being that honors the inborn gifts. For a Jane Goodall, that may mean serving humanity in a fashion that eradicates cruelty and enhances kindness to all creatures. A retired insurance executive might find "gainful employment" by mentoring young sales executives or helping new insurance firms become profitable. Generally, we feel our way into the engagements that give us the sweet satisfaction that, "Ah, I was born for this. . . ."

Parenting, teaching, clockmaking, healing—every authentic, meaningful engagement is restorative, and provides a glimpse of Eternity. That's why, like a moth diving headlong into a flame, we'll sacrifice our very life for what we love. Think this is esoteric mysticism? Think again! Our life's journey is designed to further our spiritual destiny. *That's* why we love life so much. It's that bubbling up of the living Spirit that carries us Home.

All Peace, El

P.S. BBC? Terrific stuff. *Love* it.

Did Homer float? How's Marge? How's Moo?

The Charlie Chan marathon was great fun. Next month, it's Margaret Rutherford as Miss Marple. All the old original Agatha Christie flicks are now on video, so my pals and I can watch to our heart's content.

V

The *Fifth* Exchange

~ On reviving leadership and
recovering delights ~

*No one can live
without delight,
and that is why
a man deprived
of Spiritual joy
goes over to
carnal pleasures.*

Thomas Aquinas

"I Want That Flame, That Sense That Life Is Exceedingly Worthwhile"

Dear El,

Your friend Reggie reminds me of my father, nearly one hundred when he died. He's my success-model. I admired him more than just about anyone. Much like centenarians I've read about, he overcame so much—the Great Depression and both world wars, and more. Yet my dad was serene and alert all through his living. And his dying.

We've both heard of retirees who feel miserable. They expire from sheer, blistering boredom. Contrast them with others like my father who, despite nostalgia for his former career, continued being active throughout life. Per your "emulate success models" rule of thumb, that's what I intend to do.

And why can't friends invent new rules by which to reinvent themselves? Remember that story on *60 Minutes* about a group of English society women from a tiny village who stripped naked to pose for a fund-raising project? The Calendar Girls, as they came to be known, were between mid-forty and late-sixty. They raised tons of money for charity. Beyond that, each must have confronted her fears and timidity. What guts.

We've got a lot of *"un*learning" to do!

Many of us seem like the lonely, aging character in a Woody Allen film (don't ask me which one) who's explaining why he's so isolated. In effect, he recounts his mother's warning, "Stay away from people. You'll catch their dreams." He says, as a child, he didn't see how dreams could hurt anyone, but as his mother was so worried, he took her advice. Years later, he realized she had really said, "Stay away from people, you'll catch their *germs.*" Similarly, we've learned our fears. To uncover our delights, our own reeducation is in order.

How many of us actually identify our delights? If, as Maslow proposed, the recovery of delight is a key to becoming whole, then shouldn't we emulate that Chinese scholar who listed thirty-three happy moments? For him, happiness—largely sensuous—led to the joy of the spirit. That scholar's delight included such things as drinking vast quantities of wine with old friends and hearing his children recite the classics fluently, "like the sound of pouring water from a vase," and opening a window to let a wasp out of a room. He'd sum up each happy moment by sighing, "Ah, is this not happiness?"[94] I shall start my own list of happy moments. One of which, old chum, is receiving your letters!

Do dispositions really harden over time?

My parents fit Tournier's conception of older people having two opposing dispositions. One enjoyed retirement fully, found wonderful "useful and interesting things to do," and was never, ever bored. The other conformed to Tournier's second type: was like a broken-down car, without motive power upon retiring or finding the nest empty. Is Tournier correct that "between these two extremes there are very few intermediates"? His stance is credible. He says,

> The first do not need us and our advice, and their retirement presents no problem. But how difficult

it is to advise and help the other group! The best of advice, even if it is followed, is often ineffective, because it comes from outside, without arousing much in the way of inner echo.[95]

If we agree with this, then my idea—to encourage elders in small, interactive settings—flies out the window. If, on the other hand, times have changed sufficiently and a critical mass is now ready to discuss and adopt new assumptions, education along supportive lines could stir up the inner fires. Personally, I want that flame, that sense that life is exceedingly worthwhile. That wish holds my next projects and my good news about which, in my last letter, I hoped to tell you more. Well, here it is.

The ombudsman cometh!

On my desk sits a manila folder into which I toss index cards of inspiring ideas; news clippings, cartoons, and other notable tidbits. All our letters are stuffed in there, especially as our conversations have revitalized my ambitions. Weird isn't it? Here I am, nearing seventy and I'm still hot for business!

Last month, I noticed that file is bulging. It's fat with little notes (and getting fatter). Sorting through its contents, a business concept sprang to life, full-blown: I'm all set to start something new—for elders, naturally. My plans are sketchy, but generally involve an ombudsman service for men and women in later life. *Ombudsman* originally meant "an appointed official charged with investigating reports and complaints of malfeasance by government agencies or officials against private citizens."[96] But why can't I, as ombudsman, whet people's appetite for spiritual hardiness?

I'd ask you to join me but realize you've given your heart to a contemplative life—to art, writing, and a quiet mode of teaching. Considering your vocation of solitude, I'm reminded of something Merton wrote: that contemplatives are, above all, individuals of prayer. They seek neither to renounce society nor to gain personally from their reflective life. The cloistered Christian is someone who makes of him- or herself a total gift to God, while praying for others in the process. Because few others understand this summons, the life is a real call into the unknown, and a solitary "has made a decision strong enough to be proved by the wilderness: That is to say, by death." In the end, Merton proposed, solitaries are made by God—not by man.[97] Anyhow, that's how I perceive your charter.

But enough about you. Back to my favorite topic: *Me.* Think of the assistance I might offer the elderly through advocacy in all sorts of areas, such as we've discussed:

- end-of-life care (and all the negotiations that accompany that);
- family guidance (especially intervening for the frail or infirm, should conflicts arise);
- nursing home or hospital visits (particularly if someone is recuperating slowly and requires looking in on occasionally).

And I'd see to it that all such programs become infused with positive assumptions about "old age." Later life demands the recovery of joy—identifying authentic delights—and forming relationships that restore vitality. Then there's protection from outright abuse.

Studies show us that individuals in all socioeconomic, ethnic, and religious groups are "vulnerable to abuse, but [that] the typical abuser has specific characteristics."[98] In nearly 90 percent of elder abuse and neglect the abuser was . . .

- a family member (two-thirds were adult children or spouses);
- twice as likely as nonabusers to drink heavily;
- more likely to be men or children of the victims, when substance abuse is involved.[99]

By government and other estimates, 1.5 to 2.5 million elders suffer from abuse. Given the skyrocketing increase of the elderly population in America, "the number will likely increase."[100] So that's my news: I'm back in the management education business. How sweet it is.

Heightened awareness is our first step forward.

Naturally, I'm just formulating a business plan. Before doing anything more, extensive research is required on things like training, licensing, and state and federal regulations. However, now I'm all charged up to tackle that. The opportunity to serve—and, yes, make a fair profit—seems endless. Dialogue groups, rooted in three main themes that we've raised, could be a cornerstone of support where needed most. Must I apologize for reducing our oh-so-warm encouragement to so cold a business endeavor?

Would you agree we can reduce our exchange to "Three Biggies"? Let me explain, then—please—respond.

First: *The awakening of enhanced awareness.*

We began our discussions with the agreement that we feel young as we awaken spiritually to the eternal: We are ageless at the deepest level of Reality. Our enhanced awareness and self-renewing assumptions empower us, add passion, thereby infuse us with vitality. Also, here's where I see the application for your principles for the spiritual side of aging.

We agreed that each of us can come into our own, as individuals, along some universal—by that I mean non-dogmatic—line. Vocation, side interests, and hobbies grown into meaningful commitments; connections to family and friends; lifelong learning, and the growth of our own humanity—all this can, with enhanced aware-ness, lead to "gainful employment"—that which brings purpose and fulfillment.

Second: *A changing collective context.*

As society revises its ideas on issues like "old age," "aging," "the elderly," end-of-life care, and death and dying, true dignity is now possible for those of advanced age. This mind-shift, along with its related groundswell of activism among baby boomers (and their children) will assure a new independence for people. It marks a rev-olution unlike most of what we've seen in our lifetime.

Third: *A challenged leadership.*

Leaders of every sort—corporate marketers, public policy makers, and all manner of health professionals and family members must pay attention. The sheer num-ber of elderly people—globally—who feel entitled to more honorable treatment raises the leadership bar of elder care. Surely that honorable treatment leads to the recovery of delight.

One overarching goal for leaders . . .

Earlier you asked about the impact that a graying planet might have on communities, corporations, and families. I envision one superordinate goal for leaders in every field, and particularly public-policy and public-service agencies and the helping professions, namely . . .

- to better anticipate and educate citizens for wide-scale change related to an aging population.

After hiring a few expert facilitators for my ombudsman service, I'll use our letters as a training and discourse framework. We'll need to design a curriculum for leaders. Then we'll conduct "in-house" dialogue sessions for small groups of elders. That's my first plan.

How could men and women of seventy or eighty not love an ongoing exchange such as we've had? Especially those who, after retirement, feel more is left for them to be and do. The talks need not be esoteric. I suspect people will be heartened simply by their mutual encouragement. As for me, I'm all buoyed up. Renewed. Yes, Julian of Norwich, you were right: "All is well and shall be well."

As I gear up for my enterprise—my venture of encouragement—letter writing is going to my back burner for the foreseeable future. You write. I'll phone. Okay? And, pray tell—what are *your* plans for the future?

Meanwhile, all that's good to you, Bo

P.S. Alas, Homer did float. The good news is that Marge is dandy—all rosy red and glittery. So is Moo. So's my stock portfolio!

As for the joys of antipasto, blame only yourself for the following food trivia. Ever since you mentioned "delectable Greek olives" I've experimented with varieties of fresh veggies—cleaned, sliced, then marinated in the fridge briefly before serving. My top picks? Chunks of crisp zucchini and white mushrooms; slices of ripe avocado, whole cherry tomatoes and, natch, those ever-delectable Greek olives. I pile the whole concoction on a plate, surround it with thin slices of runny Brie and firm mozzarella and rounds of sourdough bread. The marinade (olive oil, garlic slivers, balsamic vinegar, seasonings) becomes my dipping sauce for everything. Any decent wine will do. (Merlot's my new love.) *Then* I sit on the deck, and sip and munch dreamily. And marvel at the sunset. Ah, is this not happiness?

He who loves
brings God and the world
together.

Martin Buber*

*Martin Buber, *The Way of Response*, Nahum N. Glatzer, ed. (New York: Shocken Books, 1961) p. 136.

"How Might I Add Value?"

Dear B,

Wow. Something new and untried—so full of prom-ise. I'm excited: for you and, oddly, for myself. Your enthusiasm is contagious. (Wasn't it Mary Baker Eddy who said, "What blesses one, blesses all?")[101]

Yes, I prefer contemplative life. So I shall add my two cents to your venture from afar. Your recap of our "talks" triggered my own. Considering the spiritual side of later life, for me there's value only in intimacy with the divine love. That's life hidden in God—that through Christ "all things hold together in Him."[102] Turning my loyalties to that Reality is a full-time occupation. But, ah . . . is *this* not happiness?

More on that momentarily. For now, I'll rephrase the whole matter democratically: Spiritual awakening means the animation of our true selves, remembering who we are within the context of a three-pronged, totally synergistic system.

- One, we grow in *wholeness (or "integrity" of being);*
- Two, *we gain spiritual hardiness;*
- Three, *we discover our vocation or engagement.*

Our full encounter with that which quickens us at the core also reveals our distinctive place in the scheme of things. This uniqueness shapes our life with others. So there's an inner-outer blending in all this. I envision these three factors act much like an electric plug that connects us to our Source, activating whatever is eternal: spiritual attributes and, yes, delights, and the divine decree for the part we are to play in life, and the faith *of* God for actualizing that role.

"Fleshly" aging versus spiritual awakening . . .

When we think in terms of "the flesh," the problems of age seem overwhelming—even with technological advances like hip replacements and heart transplants. With a materialistic perspective, death never loses its sting. With a spiritual perspective, there's no limit to growth. Love, intuition, inspiration, or subjective delight, all these, and more, expand infinitely. The older we get, chronologically speaking, the *sharper* such attributes can be. Plus, such awakening is progressive. By paying attention to our spiritual side we can express added compassion or forgiveness at any age. You taught me that.

A few years back, you described a woman in a retirement center who, upon her ninety-seventh birthday, woke up to her abrasive nature. (If memory serves, her habit was to terrorize the care-center staff.) She realized that, before she died, she wanted to express her gratitude to those who'd cared for her despite her rudeness. She did not want to leave a legacy of hurt feelings. To me, that's love in action: the awakening of compassion or courage or *something* that subordinates *self*-interest and contributes worth.

Maturing further—beyond possessive, "personal" or even familial affection—we exhibit concern that serves the future. If, in later life, we develop in this fashion, then no matter how fragile or aching our physical state, we'll feel enveloped by an oceanic, boundless love. That love reveals all children as our children. We feel kinship with all of humankind.

When Mother Teresa visited China in the 1960s, a government official asked what she thought of Communists. She replied that they were her brothers and sisters. We may be bookish, scientific sorts—not given to showering care on our parents or neighbors—but, a boundless love will, in diverse fashion, help us bloom where we're planted.

That sort of love may confound or even anger those closest to us. A family or spouse doesn't comprehend why, for instance, we're leaving the nest for a volunteering stint in some nonprofit group or taking a loner's sail around the world or, yes, sticking close to home so we can live a contemplative life. Love calls us to Itself diversely. There's no set rule for those whose God is a consuming fire. There's no telling what we'll do.

Seen through this filter, we're not exactly aging.

We're using our spiritual journey—everything in life—our joys and hardships, to contribute something unique. The things we do each day help us become more conscious, more spiritually hardy. Spiritual hardiness, in turn, reminds us of who we really are. If we're contemplatively minded—more given to reflection than activism—then, no matter how old or infirm, our every thought furthers joy about little things.

In a recent HBO special entitled *A Century of Living,* one centenarian who was blind wept with gladness about her life. Her journey had not been easy. She'd endured losses—her sight, the deaths of parents, many other trials. Tears streamed down her cheeks as she gratefully confessed, "Life is so wonderful—I'd like to do it all over again." Gratefulness: isn't that one test of awakening?

We've agreed, all can partake of spiritual awakening by getting in touch with authentic interests—some delight, some wide love: love of home, family, or community; love of collecting antique plates, rare books, or baking sourdough bread. The more our love gets expressed tangibly, the better. The only requirement is that we be genuine in this, accepting the fact that everyone isn't called to fame like Grandma Moses or Colonel Sanders. Look at the intrinsic heroism of firefighters who give their lives while trying to save others. Do those impulses wane with age? No!

Usually, that wisdom, virtue, or genuineness expands with age. In early life, we may fault ourselves for not being more like others. In our attempt to resist, or adjust to, the whims of family or mentors, we can thwart ourselves with the choice of a spouse, career, or friendship. With added years we know better. We shrug off our people-pleasing ways or the rush to achieve everything today. A friend told me, "We live in a microwavable climate. People want all their experiences right away. Spiritual growth takes time, it meanders; the heart has its own pace."

Age teaches us it's our duty to be and do what we

love. We volunteer at the zoo or create pasta dishes because that turns us on. Gradually, we come into our own in a way that encourages our grandchildren or next-door neighbors to feel more at ease in their own skins. This, too, is love.

Simplicity balances life.

Those who chase "balance" in life—who devote twenty minutes each day to meditation, and twenty more minutes to aerobics, and one night a week to family, and another to their bridge club—may really just be craving simple being. Often they are worn out from their unrelenting busyness and over-"doing." They hunger for peace of mind, but avoid the obvious:

- a rightly ordered life;
- ongoing transcendence;
- a reoriented loyalty to the inspirations of grace.[103]

Three septuagenarians, living different lives, agreed: advanced age has increased their spirituality. One woman noticed that her genuineness grows stronger over time:

I've been married over 50 years, have grown—independently rich—children and grandchildren. I consider myself to be an artist, *being at my easel most of the time.* (I feel independent, although my husband has always supported me both financially and emotionally.)

- I think, act, and feel healthy—have never been sick.
- I'm devoted to the philosophy of my chosen religion (The Science of Mind, founded by Ernest Holmes).
- I experience daily the demonstration of the concept that "God is Love."
- I have no fear of death but consider it to be a transition.

In reading what I've written in haste, I see it sounds like my life is just one big piece of cake! Believe me—there's been a lot of ups and downs.*

Another wrote:

I am 78 and seem to cope positively with life—take no medication, and know the value of a good walk daily. (I don't always get a daily walk in, but I know its value), plus a good, nutritious diet. I try to keep

---

*Italics/underlining in original; content edited by author.

up with modern advances, but don't let the computer get me down. I play a good game of bridge and am as social as I want to be. I live alone.*

A third noted that she's always been spiritual. At age seventy-something, her love of solitude grows ever more intense. She reminded me of Einstein's remark that solitude in youth is a luxury, but in age, it becomes a necessity. This woman takes time to read inspirational books and meditate each day and spends time "just dinking around":

> I have been married 53 years, have 4 children and look "traditional." But I lead a contemplative life . . . my husband . . . pretty much does his fishing and I do my dinking around.
>   So far, that arrangement is working out fine.*

Following the patterns we've discussed, I pray each of us stays immersed in something well loved, if not several things. Not necessarily altruistic pursuits, but activities born of enough affection to lift the mind "out" of its

---

*Letter edited by author.

mundane ruts—its self-interests, its aches, its worries. Only in our high center of thought do we pass over feelings of separateness and enter the rare healing realms of an awakening, joyful heart.[104]

Remember author Norman Cousins' superb illustration of such curative realms? Cousins visited Albert Schweitzer at his hospital in Lambarine, after the renowned doctor was in his nineties. Cousins observed "human purpose bordering on the supernatural." Schweitzer handled his rounds with intense devotion, did "strenuous carpentry," moved heavy crates of medicine with "all his multiple skills . . . energized by a torrential drive to use his mind and body."[105] He believed that so long as he had "a job to do and a good sense of humor," no disease could find a home in his body. Now there's a healthy assumption.

Schweitzer loved music. He played daily on one of two old, upright pianos left untuned for years and subjected to the heat and humidity of the tropics. Yet, as Schweitzer played, Cousins felt "a stronger sense of listening to a great console than if [he] had been in the world's largest cathedral. . . ."[106] After playing his favorite piece (Bach's Toccata and Fugue in D Minor) Schweitzer appeared "restored" and "enhanced." He stood up and "there was no trace of stoop. Music was his medicine."[107]

That's the heart posture and the focus that heals—the divine or beautiful *object* of attention that fuels hope and renews us physically.

The monastic tradition speaks of "self-vanishing," wherein awareness expands into an ineffable state, beyond our persona or "mask." Music and work prompted Schweitzer's self-vanishing. This means he communed with something larger than himself with rapt attention— which is one face of love. I can't repeat this too often. This communion could be sparked by almost anything—working the *New York Times* crossword puzzle or riding our ten-speed along a lonely beach path. As we identify with the joy or peace of that experience, a delicate harmony may overtake us, not simply as an abstracted "value" to discuss intellectually, but as direct experience. Now we enter an "ineffable sweetness," as the saintly Henry Suso once observed. This, the key to health, is what we crave.

Life gives us repeated chances, years and years of chances, to unite with the love that heals. The great life-lovers, such as St. Francis of Assisi or Albert Schweitzer, begin their spiritual journeys by taking small steps. Bit by bit, their pilgrimage leads to a wider love. Our delights can lead us. So can what we call "losses."

Don't forget that wonderful tale of the monk whose brother kept stealing all his money: The thefts persisted daily, for years, until the thieving brother was dying. Then he begged for forgiveness. Whereupon the monk kissed his brother's hands and feet and cried, "Oh, no forgiveness is needed—for you have taught me how to be a true monk."

Everything and everyone is our teacher.

Yes, I'm advancing in the contemplative life you so aptly described in your last missive. That's my gainful employment, my own move from death to life. These days, each experience and failing teaches me that transition is marked not so much by seeking or achieving as by resting in that Light which is our life. But never fear; mine is no hermit's destiny. Together, we shall still celebrate our glazed duck at Thanksgiving, and exchange red scarves and books at Christmas. And chat on the phone.

The trick is to express ourselves fruitfully *from* that place which is uniquely ours to inhabit: from our talent, vocation, or prayer. That place is a trust—a spiritual commission; an assignment, if you will.

Perhaps you'll say, "Well, nothing new here." But doesn't fruitfulness require each active life to somehow commune with God? And ask each secluded life to take an active, grateful part in bringing Creation to fulfillment.[108] In that sense, the things we're born to do find us. Which brings me to my own plans.

"How might I add value . . . ?"

I long to approach some potent service from a transformed heart. How, I wonder, might I *be* and *do* all things in a way that unites God and man? God is ever at hand. But most of us are so distracted, so absent from Reality. Since thought precedes action, perhaps I can add value by lifting human thought to God's.

For we are God's idea, God's poem of love, and quickened only by the divine love. In proportion as we turn toward God's thoughts, which are higher than ours, we even inhale Love's fragrance with our last mortal breath.

My idea of success these days, is to love brother, neighbor, and friend as myself, and to love God above all else. Of course, humanly, it's impossible. Of myself I cannot do this. I feel like the monk in that story where a guest, visiting a monastery, asks, "What do you monks do all day with so much time on your hands?" Whereupon the monk answers, "Well, we get up in the morning, intending to be pure and good and loving. Then we fall down. So we get up. Then we fall. We get up again. Then we fall again. That is how we spend our time."

Since that pretty much sums up my virtue, I lean on Mother Teresa's advice: Success is not our primary objective; being *faithful* is our main job.

With this in mind, here's my grand plan . . .

I intend to pray and write, and teach and draw, and preach and putter in ways that bring God and the world together. That noble course starts with me. Ultimately, the lion must lay down with the lamb in my *own* heart. That's full time work. It includes "casting the burden." When I reach my limits, I'm turning matters over to God.

This emerging awareness includes awe, the knowing—grateful—receptivity to what is beyond time. The toast I butter, the *Requiem* I hear, why even the person whom I appear consciously to avoid—all this feels fabulously prearranged. In that sense, there's so little to do.

And here's a paradox: Though I aim to encourage others, that job is not about changing, teaching, "improving," or enlightening anyone—not even myself. It's enough to witness, to share my experience, to say that life in God is already divine. That, here and now, we're living out from that point—neither struggling to ignore shadows nor forcing ourselves to look up to the stars, but actually gazing out *from* our encounter of Emmanuel— God with us—in Christ, *alive and sealed with us, as us.*[109]

Ultimately, spiritual awakening at any age is a grace. Not a willful thing at all. More and more we simply come awake in God's presence, find that all our doings— our comings and goings—occur in the awareness that we are already engrossed with what will be our occupation in eternity.[110] It's so beautiful it takes my breath away.

So, you build a compassionate human service business, and I'll stick to my contemplative writing-teaching life: I'll prune the pink vine roses that blanket my arbor, and sweep dead leaves from my deck, and scrub copper pots till they shine. And boil green beans for supper; yes, and write books and paint pictures and more—all that, while resting in a heart-prayer that sighs along with mystic Meister Eckhart, "God and I, we are one . . . one in this is-ness, eternally performing one work, for this 'he' who is God and this 'I' which is the soul are greatly fruitful."[111] Thus shall each gritty task let me live gladly. Thus, centered in God, shall I live on.

Thinking such thoughts, I awoke this dawn with an old song floating about in mind—the one Maurice Chevalier sang, about each day being like a step in a long stairway leading to Paradise. While sipping a cup of green tea, humming that tune under my breath, promptly the realization struck: Many of us—so many over this lovely blue planet—are no longer aiming for Paradise. To be most precise, after a certain point of awakening, we finally realize: We *are* Paradise.

Now, dear heart, isn't this the shift of mind over which the choirs of angels rejoice?

All Peace, El

P.S. Yes, you call. I'll write. And kiss little Moo for me, and sweet Marge with the glistening orange-red fins.

Appendices

All which thy child's mistake
Fancies is lost, I have stored for thee at home;
Rise, clasp My hand, and come!

Francis Thompson,
"The Hound of Heaven"[112]

A Word to the Reader

☙

Just as weeding, pruning, and mulching stimulate a garden's growth, so honest reflection on experience can promote human development. The following studies and general questions invite further, more specific, exploration into the concepts discussed in the text. By articulating your own insights about later life (from the vantage point of direct experience, observation, and relations with friends, family and community) the questions provided might stimulate specifics related to your own "awakening."

Consider working individually or, perhaps, in a small study group expedited by a qualified facilitator.

Furthermore, as this book's narrative suggests, it is entirely likely that gerontologists and counselors with college, corporate, and counseling purposes, as well as trusted friends, both distant and near, can utilize this appendix to initiate a dialogue on spirituality and age. May we all extend our leadership and "self-leadership" reach, while expanding understanding about the subtly nuanced awakenings of later life. This, too, is love.

Appendix A

Exchange II

Among the many shifts in awareness that Bo and El explore in this set of exchanges are such things as: the power of thought; mutual encouragement; positive rebellion—the ability to speak up for what they value; overcoming ageist assumptions, and preparing for a greatly extended life span (including work or "gainful employment" as defined by the friends).

As you consider this set of exchanges, you may want to identify your own unique links between spirituality and longevity.

⌒ Stories to Stimulate Thought

Later life requires us to create new choices, stories, vocabularies, and identifications. Those who can't—or won't—often end up feeling invisible! For example, for

---

several years, the author served as a corporate advisor to an illumined consortium of Japanese and American entrepreneurs. The elite group was researching the potentials of building an upscale retirement facility in California. The firm recruited a world-class team of architects, educators, and gerontologists and asked them to contribute ideas to this R & D project.

During that lengthy period, the author met with life-care specialists from other nations, including Sweden and Japan. The latter explained—in metaphorical terms—how they treated the infirmities of age, for instance what Westerners call Alzheimer's disease:

> Some of us consider advanced age, including its seeming declines, as a "sacred" state. When the individual has learned enough from this world, and perhaps as preparation for the next, he or she may "vacate" the human mind/body, moving into a holy space—one without human memory or obligation. As helping professionals, our group feels it's our job, our privilege, to serve these individuals, to protect and nurture them as best we can. Never to exploit, demean, or torment, as is sometimes done. We've learned that our own salvation now depends on our righteous service in this domain.

Over the next few months, as you and your associates consider the ideas, values, and assumptions of later life, you might consider questions like these:

- How do you respond to ageist propaganda from authority figures, such as family doctors and health-care practitioners?
- How clearly do you teach others—family and friends—to treat you?
- To what extent are you a "good steward of the soul"?
- What does that last phrase mean to you in terms of your own awakening, your own aging?

- To what extent do you sense that language and the identifications and metaphors of aging might create new models for your own joyful longevity?
- As you consider how you might contribute to the revision of obsolete ageist notions (its stories and language) what specific changes would you like to see in adult education programs or health-care attitudes and offerings?

- What's your definition of "gainful employment"?
- Who in your circle of associates has successfully revised

a working life after so-called retirement, and what conclusions do you draw from such examples?

- What does "spiritual awakening" mean to you?
- Who would you most like to engage in a dialogue on such issues? Why?
- In your opinion, how might the arts—dance; painting; sculpting; community theater; music—fit into our local, national, and international conversations? How might you lend leadership to such dialogues?

Exchange III

This series of exchanges relates to friendships, assertion, and spiritual hardiness in later life. Many practical concerns crop up, including issues of self-leadership and reinvention.

Over the next few months, as you and your associates consider the ideas, values, and assumptions of later life, you might consider questions like these:

- What aspects of spiritual awakening—e.g., finding meaning; forgiving old hurts and oneself; contributing one's gifts in some fashion; learning new skills;

adopting new role models, clothes, friendships, lifestyles for oneself, etc.—might restore the sense of revived purpose?

- In your opinion how might the issues of spiritual awakening add value to our social life? (E.g., joining new study groups? Reaching out to new friends? Helping others extend themselves variously?)

- Have you learned to say "yes" and "no" as if you mean it, for whatever you need? To what extent is such assertiveness an awakening (or part of our "spiritual work") and why?
- Have you identified and spoken up for what's of value to you?
- Have you learned to hear what's of value to others?
- Here again, how might sports, or the arts—e.g., yoga classes; storytelling; creating new mythologies, heroes and heroines for later life, etc.—and the contemplative arts (prayer, prayer circles; meditation; journaling, etc.) help older people reinvent themselves, encourage and be encouraged, and stay connected to others?
- What other activities could enhance spiritual awakening that you might "finish your course with joy"? (Acts 20:24)

Exchange IV

This round of exchanges underscores the creaking underbelly of old age: its frailties; its death and dying—topics no one has wanted to discuss. We note that certain habits of mind, relatedness, and vital engagement help people transcend what Jung may have called the disengaged psyche—that season of transition, when people either cling to temporal dead ends or find new life in the eternal verities. Like El, those who identify with spiritual realties gain (as both Jung and Joseph Campbell have pointed out) "structuring power." Instead of feeling like society's ghosts, they find freedom in the relinquishments of age.

Over the next months, as you and your associates explore the ideas, values, and assumptions of later life; you might consider questions like these:

- What sorts of older people inspire your own vision for your later years and why?
- What habits of mind, relatedness, or engagement make those you admire seem so robust or fully functioning? What is it that animates their life?
- Why do you admire these individuals—which of their character traits spark your interest? What might that mean?

- What are they doing with their lives that you'd like to do?
- What is the spiritual "vision" or path that these archetypes (or role models) sanctify, honor, or represent?

⌁ Stories to Stimulate Thought

Before reflecting on death and dying, you may find it helpful to read Dorothy Day's touching account of lessons learned about death from one Father Roy. For example, his words about the suffering of a Russian man, to whom death came slowly, could provide comfort to those not used to considering such transitions.[113]

Consider, too, the many heroes and heroines aboard American flights attacked by terrorists on September 11, 2001. In a well-publicized account, one young man sensing he and fellow passengers were about to die, phoned GTE on his cell phone (when he couldn't reach his wife). He told the operator what was happening and asked her to pray the Lord's Prayer with him. As his wife later recounted, he then sought help from Jesus, "and once he got that guidance he asked [the operator] to contact me . . . and to tell us how much he loved us. Then once he had all that business squared away, he apparently jumped the hijacker [who was] wearing a bomb, thus preventing the plane from heading into the Capitol.[114]

Then there's the consoling story of a man who came home late one night, walking in on a burglar. The thief proceeded to beat the homeowner senseless. The thief ran way, leaving the man floating in and out of consciousness. Neighbors found him, called the ambulance, and while this was going on the man had a near-death experience. Later he told friends, "I don't remember feeling any pain—only the most incredible love washing over me."

The fairy tale, the myth, the parable, the true story— these encode consciousness, educate for possibilities, lift thought (and spirit) higher that we might meet life's next assignments boldly, fearlessly, and with heart.

Over the next months, as you and your associates explore the ideas, values, and assumptions of later life; you might consider questions like these:

• In your opinion, what other stories might help us "walk our talk" or live courageously and beautifully even in the face of death and dying?

- What sorts of dialogue, education, and spiritual direction might help you gain strength for later life? Why?
- How might a community (or family, church, synagogue, friends) help you talk more openly about death and dying? Why?
- How might a community (or friends, church, synagogue, etc.) assist its elderly to achieve a "dignified passing"? What exactly does that phrase mean to you? If you feel our death and dying is no one's business but our own—that it's a private matter and the less said the better—what public policies might you propose for the community/health-care practices you'd support?

- What has been your own direct experience, say, in your closest circle, with death and how has that experience colored your thoughts to these questions?
- How might end-of-life care be improved in your local setting?
- To what extent do your aging relatives and friends still work, learn, or involve themselves in community life? What might others learn from them?
- A focus on spiritual awakening in later life could well ask you to redefine words like *success*. What might *success* mean to you after age sixty-five, eighty-five, ninety-five?

Exchange V

Throughout their last exchanges, the two friends attempt to reevaluate the spiritual awakening, the engagements, and the relationships of later life.

Over the next months, as you and your associates consider your own revision, you might consider questions like these:

- How would you sum up your own spiritual aspirations for later life? That is, what sorts of life skills, ideals, values, friendships, or "gainful employment" might lift your thought, your spirit?
- To what extent are you and your friends consciously addressing such "work"—the spiritual awakenings of adult life?
- How relevant are the themes of spiritual awakening and mutual encouragement to you? Why?

Appendix B

If times have changed sufficiently and a
critical mass is now ready to discuss and adopt
new assumptions, then education along supportive
lines could stir up the inner fires.

"Bo"
The Fifth Exchange

Now for some longevity facts for those of you who enjoy delving a bit deeper into a few readily available figures:

Longevity

- The proportion of those over eighty-five will quadruple by the year 2050.
- One in nine current baby boomers will live to at least ninety. If we're alive in the year 2020, there's a good chance we'll live to 120.
- Centenarians are the fastest growing segment of society, worldwide.

Work

- New laws already allow us to work after age sixty-five without forgoing social security benefits.
- Over two million workers between the ages of sixty and sixty-five are currently in the workforce. These folks appear to be healthier than those who withdraw from life.
- According to Sam Ervin's article in *The Futurist*, compared to the gainfully employed, "non-working seniors are more likely to have significant health and daily living problems."[115]

Connection√

- Seventy percent of those asked say they miss the social life they had before retiring, A Harris Poll reported that among those in their sixties, over half of those interviewed feel the loss of their usual roles.[116]

- Those who have little contact with friends and relatives and/or who don't belong to a place of worship have about a third higher increased risk of death.

Healing Choice√

Related to simple assertion, many practical habits appear to either enhance or diminish well being in later life. For instance:

- Frailty in old age may be the inevitable result of *years* of living with unhealthy ideas and choices.

- Elderly smokers have an increased risk of death (as compared to those who never smoked).

- Those who are sixty and older who exercise infrequently face a higher death risk than those who exercise regularly.

In terms of the group called hardy elders . . .

- Sixty-nine percent use the Internet and read avidly.

- Forty-one percent still work and are committed to friends and family.
- Two-thirds, despite chronic diseases, control their diseases, rather than letting their illnesses control them, and they take care of their own affairs.[117]

Dignity in Later Life

- According to an AARP survey, about 81 percent of those polled "claim to have given considerable thought to retirement [and] say they feel optimistic about those years.[118]
- A growing consumer trend is the demand for a dignified passing. Bill and Judith Moyer's innovative PBS documentary, *On Our Own Terms*, revealed that 80 percent of Americans now want to die at home. That desire transcends mere mass opinion. It's a rising tide, a collective feeling of entitlement of "Why can't we have this?"[119]
- Only 5.2 percent of older people live in nursing homes.
- Older people maintain curiosity and are capable learners.
- Fully one-third of America's elderly currently work for pay; many of them support families and friends; another third work as volunteers.[120]

Notes

1. Philippians 4:7.
2. Psalm 23.
3. Song of Solomon 2:10–11.
4. Paul Tillich, *The Courage to Be* (New Haven: Yale University Press, 1952).
5. Song of Solomon 2:11–13.
6. Thomas Merton, *Thoughts in Solitude* (New York: Farrar, Straus and Giroux, 1958), p. 83.
7. Julian of Norwich, *Revelations of Divine Love* (New York: Penguin Books, 1966).
8. Neville Goddard, *The Power of Awareness* (Marina Del Rey, Calif.: DeVorss Publications, 1952), p. 64.
9. Evelyn Underhill, *Mysticism* (New York: E. P. Dutton, Inc., 1961), pp. 370–71, 477.
10. Isaiah 55:12.
11. John Cantwell-Kiley, *Self-Rescue* (Los Angeles: Lowell House, 1990, 1992), p. 43.
12. Joel 3:10.
13. Etta Clark, *Growing Old Is Not for Sissies: Portraits of Senior Athletes* (Corte Madera, Calif.: Pomegranate Calendars and Books, 1986), p. 111.
14. "Looking Ahead, a Baby-Boomer Perspective," AARP, 10/9/2000, www.usinfo.state.gov/journals/itsv.0699/ijse/aarp.html.

15. John Hargreaves, *As "I" See It* (Carmel, Calif.: Mulberry Press, 1999).
16. Song of Solomon, 2:11–14.
17. Nehemiah 8:10.
18. Lionel Tiger, *Optimism* (New York: Simon and Schuster, 1979).
19. Mark 9:23.
20. Art Linkletter, *Old Age Is Not for Sissies: Choices for Senior Americans* (New York: Penguin Books, 1989), pp. 140–41.
21. http://www.graypanthers.org/info:/htm.
22. David Redding, "The Serenity Prayer," in *Positive Thinking* (Guideposts Publication, Jan.–Feb. 2001, v. 52, #1, Pt. 11), p. 18.
23. Rollo May, *Man's Search for Himself* (New York: W.W. Norton; Signet Books, 1953), p. 8.
24. Robert Bolt, *Man for All Seasons* (New York: Scholastic Books, 1960).
25. Randi Henderson, *The Gifts of Age* (Common Boundary, September–October 1995), pp. 28–31 (paraphrased by author).
26. *CNN Moneyline News Hour*, "Retirement Can Wait," CNN, Nov. 23, 2000; transcript, federal documents, no page number.
27. Salvatore R. Maddi and Suzanne C. Kobasa, *The Hardy Executive*, Health Under Stress (Chicago: Dorsey Professional Books, 1984).
28. Ibid.
29. Sarah L. Delany and A. Elizabeth Delany with Amy Hill Hearth, *Having Our Say* (New York: Dell Books, 1993), p. 293.
30. Ibid, pp. 288–89.
31. Sogyal Rinpoche, *Glimpse After Glimpse: Daily Reflections on Living & Dying* (San Francisco: Harper San Francisco, 1995), March 22 (no page number).

32. Abishiktananda, *Prayer* (New Delhi, India: ISPCK, 1993 ed.), p. 29.
33. Hebrews 3:11.
34. Revelation 21:6.
35. Job 24:13–16.
36. Malachi 3:10.
37. Thomas Szasz, *The Untamed Tongue* (LaSalle, Ill.: Open Court Publishing, 1990), p. 147.
38. Rollo May, *The Courage to Create* (New York: Bantam Books; W. W. Norton, 1975), p. 3.
39. Malcolm Cowley, *The View from Eighty* (New York: Viking Press, 1980), pp. 16–17, 68.
40. Evelyn Underhill, *Mysticism* (New York: E. P. Dutton, 1961), p. 237.
41. Anthony de Mello, *One Minute Wisdom* (New York: Doubleday Image, 1985), p. 83.
42. Martha Wilcox, *The Power of a Divine Idea* (booklet) (Santa Clara, Calif.: The Bookmark, no date provided), p. 1.
43. Malcolm Cowley, op. cit., p. 48.
44. Salvatore R. Maddi and Suzanne C. Kobasa, op. cit., pp. 30–31.
45. Ibid.
46. Marsha Sinetar, *Spiritual Intelligence* (New York: Orbis Books, 2000).
47. John Briggs, *Fire in the Crucible* (Los Angeles: Jeremy P. Tarcher, 1990).
48. Laurie Lisle, *Portrait of an Artist: A Biography of Georgia O'Keeffe* (New York: Washington Square Press, Pocket Books, 1981), p. 244.
49. Ibid., p. 434.
50. Paraphrased from the original story in Anthony de Mello, op. cit., p. 157.
51. Sam L. Ervin, "Fourteen Forecasts for an Aging Society," *The Futurist*, Nov./Dec. 2000, pp. 24–28.

52. Ibid.
53. Burrell's Information Services, NBC, *Today*, June 15, 2000, pp. 20–21. Dr. Mike Magee's outline of Pfizer's "Pulse Study" can also be found in this source.
54. Leonard Orr and Sondra Ray, *Rebirthing in the New Age* (Millbrae, Calif.: Celestial Arts, 1977), ch. 6.
55. Marsha Sinetar, *Ordinary People As Monks and Mystics* (Mahwah, N.J.: Paulist Press, 1986), ch. 8.
56. Abraham Maslow, *Toward a Psychology of Being* (Princeton, N.J.: D. Van Nostrand, Insight Books, 1962), pp. 110, 118.
57. Ibid., p. 118.
58. *Diagnosis Murder*, CBS, episode of June 23, 2001.
59. Marsha Sinetar, *Spiritual Intelligence* (Maryknoll, N.Y.: Orbis Books, 2000), p. 10.
60. De Mello, op. cit., p. 34.
61. Albert Einstein, *The World As I See It*, Alan Harris, trans. (Philosophical Library, n.d.), p. 2.
62. C. G. Jung, *Memories, Dreams, Reflections* (New York: Vintage Books, 1965), p. 302.
63. Champion Teutsch, *Joel's Revelations* (Pittsburgh, Pa.: Dorrance, 1993), p. 32.
64. John W. Gardner, *Excellence: Can We Be Equal and Excellent Too?* (New York: Harper Colophon Books, 1961), pp. 159–60.
65. Steve Wall and Harvey Arden, *WisdomKeepers: Meetings with Native American Spiritual Elders* (Hillsboro, Oregon: Beyond Words Publishing, 1990), p. 51.
66. John Cloud, "A Kinder, Gentler Death," *Time*, Sept. 18, 2000, pp. 62–65.
67. Ibid., p. 64.
68. Ibid., pp. 62–65.
69. Ibid., p. 65.
70. Art Linkletter, op. cit., p. 137.

71. Anonymous, *A Spiritual Friendship* (New York: Crossroad, 1999), p. 72. Bracketed text paraphrased by author.
72. Paul Tournier, *Learn to Grow Old* (New York: Harper and Row; London: SCM Press Ltd., 1972), p. 18.
73. Rollo May, *Man's Search for Himself* (New York: W. W. Norton, 1953), p. 137. Italics in original.
74. Susan Nolen-Hoehsema, Ph.D., and Carla Graysen, Ph.D., "Explaining the Gender Differences in Depressive Symptoms," *California Journal of Personality and Social Psychology*, vol. 77, no. 5 (in http://www.altmedicine.com/app/archive).
75. Florence Scovel Shinn, *The Secret Door to Success* (Marina Del Rey, Calif.: DeVorss Publications, 1940), p. 30.
76. John 5:24; Jeremiah 21:8.
77. John 8:21, 24.
78. Anonymous, *A Spiritual Friendship*, p. 99.
79. Thomas Merton, *The New Man* (New York: Farrar, Straus and Giroux, 1961), pp. 246–48.
80. Ibid.
81. Elisabeth Kübler-Ross, *Living with Death and Dying* (New York: Macmillan, Collier Books, 1981), p. 48.
82. See Deuteronomy 33:27.
83. Malachi 3:2–5.
84. Florida Scott-Maxwell, *The Measure of My Days* (New York: Penguin Group, Viking, 1979 ed.), p. 91.
85. Ibid., p. 95.
86. Ibid., p. 119.
87. Etta Clark, op. cit., p. 111.
88. Robert S. Wood, *Peaceful Passing* (Sedona, Ariz.: In Print Publishing, 2000), pp. 200–202.
89. Gwen Robyns, *The Mysteries of Agatha Christie: An Intimate Biography of the First Lady of Crime* (Middlesex, U.K.: Penguin, 1978), p. 142.
90. Ibid., p. 257.

91. Christopher F. Monte, *Beneath the Mask* (New York: Praeger, 1977), p. 375.

92. Malcolm Cowley, op. cit., p. 51.

93. Jane Goodall with Phillip Berman, *Reason for Hope: A Spiritual Journey* (New York: Warner Books, 1999), pp. 243–42. Italics in original.

94. Lin Yutang, *The Importance of Living* (New York: Capricorn Books, 1937), p. 134.

95. Paul Tournier, op. cit., pp. 117–18.

96. *New Webster's Dictionary of the English Language*, College Edition, p. 1035.

97. Thomas Merton, *Thoughts in Solitude*, pp. 101–3.

98. Nelba Chaves, Ph.D., and Ruth Sanchas-Way, Ph.D., "Violence Against the Elderly, " CSAP Resource Guide, IPRC INFOSITE, http://www.drugs,indiana.edu/edu/publications/neadi/raar/rguides/MS719.html.

99. Ibid.

100. Ibid.

101. Mary Baker Eddy, *Science and Health with Key to the Scriptures* (Christian Science Board of Directors, 1971 ed.), 206:16.

102. Colossians 1:15–17.

103. Marsha Sinetar, *Sometimes, Enough Is Enough* (New York: Harper Collins, Cliff St. Books, 2000), p. 6.

104. Proverbs 17:22.

105. Norman Cousins, *Anatomy of an Illness* (New York: W. W. Norton, 1979), p. 79.

106. Ibid., pp. 79–82.

107. Ibid., pp. 79–82.

108. Abishiktananda, *Prayer* (New Delhi, India: ISPCK, 1993), ch. 5 and p. 47.

109. 2 Corinthians 1:21–22.

110. The author wishes to acknowledge Abishiktananda (op. cit.) for this idea of our having "an occupation in eternity."

111. *Meister Eckhart*, Edmund Colledge and Bernard McGinn, eds., Classics of Western Spirituality (Mahwah, N.J.: Paulist Press, 1981), pp. 188–208.

112. Francis Thompson, "The Hound of Heaven" (public domain).

113. Dorothy Day, *The Long Loneliness* (New York: Harper and Row, 1952), pp. 247–60.

114. CNN *Larry King Live*, Sept. 18, 2001, Cable News Network, Transcripts, Federal Documents Clearing House, pp. 7–8.

115. Sam L. Ervin's article, "Fourteen Forecasts for an Aging Society," in *The Futurist,* is a fine reference tool for those who work in health-care related fields.

116. "Perspectives in Health Promotion & Aging," vol. 10, no. 1, 1995, NEIHP; AARP; Washington, D.C.

117. Ibid.

118. http://www.usinfo.state.gov/journals/itsv/0699/ijse/aarp. htm.

119. Bill Moyers and Judith Moyers, *On Our Own Terms*, Public Broadcasting System (pbs.org/onourownterms/).

120. Hospice Foundation of America, "What Is Hospice?" (http://www.hospicefoundation.org/virtual—html/whatis hospicehtm).

Indexes

General Subject Index

General Name Index